The Hunt for

Hidden
Killers

THE HUNT FOR
HIDDEN KILLERS

*Ten Cases of
Medical Mystery*

Diane Yancey

*The Millbrook Press
Brookfield, Connecticut*

Photos courtesy of: UPI/Bettmann: pp. 17, 63; Photo Researchers: pp. 22 (CDC/Science Source), 30 (Scott Camazine), 36 (© John Bova, 1981), 54 (Alexander Lowry), 74 (© Ulrike Welsch, 1987), 78, (© Geoffrey Gove), 86 (Biophoto Associates/Science Source), 95 (Porterfield/Chickering); National Library of Medicine: p. 39; Centers for Disease Control: p. 47; Reuters/Bettmann: p. 50; Bettmann Archive: p.71; American Lung Association: p. 82; Harvey Finkle, Impact Visuals: p. 101.

Library of Congress Cataloging-in-Publication Data
Yancey, Diane.
The hunt for hidden killers: ten cases of medical mystery / by Diane Yancey.
p.   cm.
Includes bibliographical references and index.
Summary: Describes how doctors and public health investigators work to unravel the mysteries surrounding unusual symptoms, unexplained poisonings, and outbreaks of rare or previously unknown diseases.
ISBN 1-56294-389-8
1. Epidemiology—Juvenile literature. [1. Epidemiology.] I. Title.
RA653.5.Y35   1994
614.4—dc20   93-16638   CIP   AC

Published by The Millbrook Press
2 Old New Milford Road, Brookfield, Connecticut 06804

All of the people and events in
the mysteries are real, although
the names of some of the victims
have been changed.

Contents

The Hunt for

Hidden
Killers

Introduction

The Detectives

Dr. Joseph McDade peered into his microscope and adjusted the focus so the image was sharp and clear. At his left hand lay a box of slides he had already checked. On his right, a formidable pile awaited his attention.

The lab around him was silent. Most of his co-workers were home, taking a well-earned Christmas break.

Not McDade. In the past six months, twenty-nine lives had been lost in a mysterious epidemic. After a long and intense investigation, the cause remained unknown. McDade had already spent countless hours in the lab, reviewing these same slides. Nothing had looked suspicious.

Refusing to be beaten, he had returned today, grimly determined to track down the elusive killer. What was it? Where had it come from?

He discarded one slide, slipped in another, and scanned the surface millimeter by tiny millimeter. He didn't know what he was looking for, but it had to be there. It had to.

He stopped, stared at the slide, rubbed his eyes, and focused more carefully. This was it.

There was no mistaking what he saw . . .

•••••

Joseph McDade was no ordinary doctor. He was a "disease detective," one of a renowned group of men and women who work for the most influential disease-fighting agency in the United States, the Centers for Disease Control and Prevention (known as the Centers for Disease Control until October 1992, and still identified by the initials CDC).

The CDC, created during World War II to protect U.S. soldiers from malaria, is located on the outskirts of Atlanta, Georgia. It has several branches across the country, many of them associated with state public health departments.

Inside its headquarters, investigators like McDade go about the business of solving some of the most baffling mysteries of modern medicine. A few work in labs to learn the secrets of deadly organisms such as those that cause Lassa and Ebola fevers. Others, the "shoe-leather scientists," prefer life in the field, tracking contagious diseases such as tuberculosis and cholera.

CDC sleuths like McDade were involved in many of the cases in this book, but they are not the only medical detectives to unravel mysteries. In some chapters, county and state health department workers are the heroes, pursuing clues and uncovering evidence with thoroughness and determination. In other episodes, the investigators are doctors in hospitals and private practices across the country, "hooked" on a case by an extraordinary need or a unique set of circumstances.

Whether the medical detectives are CDC scientists or family doctors, they share qualities that uniquely equip them for their tasks: an inquiring medical mind, a desire to ease human suffering, and a determination to beat even the worst odds.

When these qualities bring them head to head with the mysteries, they tune up their intellects and polish their investigating skills.

The hunt for hidden killers begins.

Chapter

1

Killer at
the Bellevue
Stratford

In the state of Pennsylvania, men were mysteriously dying, and no one knew why.

The problem started on Thursday, July 23, 1976. Three days earlier, more than ten thousand American Legionnaires, members of the largest veterans' organization in the United States, had gathered in Philadelphia for their annual four-day state convention.

Many of the Legionnaires stayed at the Bellevue Stratford Hotel, one of Philadelphia's oldest and showiest landmarks. Between meetings, banquets, and dances in the crystal and gilt public rooms, the visitors enjoyed sightseeing, baseball games, and the city's theaters and nightclubs.

On the night of July 23, Sam Morris, a forty-eight-year-old Legionnaire, decided to skip dinner. He felt sick, sick enough to leave the convention early the next morning and go straight to bed when he got home. By Monday, Sam had a high fever. He called his family doctor, Ernest Campbell, who sent him to the hospital and ordered tests to identify the illness.

At the hospital, Dr. Campbell received disturbing news. Two of Sam's convention buddies were also patients there, showing the same symptoms as Sam. Suspecting a possible epidemic, Dr. Campbell notified the state health department.

The health department was already alerted to the Legionnaires' plight. A call from Williamsport, fifty miles away, had reported that six more men from the convention had checked into a hospital with high fevers.

On Tuesday, July 27, the first death occurred.

By Monday, August 2, more than 50 cases had been reported (later tallies would show that more than 150 people had actually fallen ill by this date). Some men, like Sam, seemed likely to recover; others were not so lucky. The death toll stood at eight and was rising hourly.

Following required procedure, state health department officials notified the Centers for Disease Control (CDC) in Atlanta, Georgia. The CDC moved quickly. Within hours, three doctors were on their way to Philadelphia to begin the hunt for the killer.

Dr. David Fraser, a slender man in his mid-thirties, was in charge of the investigation. Fraser had worked for two years as an Epidemic Intelligence Service (EIS) officer with the CDC. Now he pulled together the team he would need: EIS officers, state public health officers, Philadelphia police, secretaries, and telephone operators—more than 150 people in all.

Although they had few clues to the illness they were tracking, the investigators agreed on a rough definition of the symptoms: a cough and fever of 102°F (39°C) or higher, or any fever with a chest X ray that showed the patient had pneumonia. The victims also

From the outside, the Bellevue Stratford looked like any other luxury hotel. But inside, hotel guests were stricken with a mysterious lethal illness.

had to have some connection with the American Legion convention or the Bellevue Stratford Hotel.

In their headquarters, Fraser stuck up a map with yellow pins to mark cases, red pins to mark deaths. By the end of the first full day of work, more than seventy cases were confirmed. Eighteen red pins reminded the team that there was no time to waste. The illness had to be identified and a cure found as quickly as possible.

The EIS specialists soon lived up to their nickname, the "shoe-leather scientists." They spent days on their feet, visiting hospitals, hotels, and restaurants, asking themselves "where"—where had the Legionnaires come in contact with the disease?

First they interviewed the sick. Those strong enough to talk answered endless questions. Where did you stay at the convention? What activities did you attend? Whom did you talk to? Where and what did you eat? When did you first feel sick?

At the same time, other investigators took samples of carpets, wallpaper, curtains, ice machines, food, and drink from the Bellevue Stratford. The plumbing, air-conditioning, and kitchen equipment were tested. In the hotel's neighborhood, the investigators checked birds, animals, restaurants, street vendors—anything the victims might have encountered in common.

While the shoe-leather scientists did their work, laboratory scientists analyzed blood, urine, and saliva samples from sick Legionnaires and tissue samples from the dead. They hoped to answer the question "what"—what caused "Legion fever" (as Legionnaires' disease was originally called)? They looked at two general categories: toxic substances such as poisons, and infectious organisms such as bacteria, fungi, and viruses.

The nature of the illness seemed to rule out toxins. Many of the victims had fevers of 105°F (40.5°C) or higher. Poisons that caused high fevers usually had a strange taste or a foul odor. They would have been noticed.

Bacteria, viruses, and similar microorganisms were more likely answers. The scientists began the time-consuming task of looking for and eliminating diseases that ranged from blastomycosis and histoplasmosis (fungus infections) to typhoid and bubonic plague (caused by deadly bacteria), from mumps and measles (illnesses caused by viruses) to Rocky Mountain Spotted Fever (an infection caused by rickettsias, small, specialized types of bacteria).

All the while, more Legionnaires were getting sick and dying. Newspapers spread the story across the nation. The public panicked. Rooms at the Bellevue Stratford emptied and stayed empty. Conventions scheduled at the hotel were canceled. (Three months later, on November 18, 1976, the Bellevue Stratford went out of business, another victim of Legionnaires' disease.)

Concerned calls poured in. At first, the investigators tried to handle the uproar personally. Dr. Fraser spent days answering phone calls and reporters' questions. "It was an environment in which it was hard to do science—or anything else!" he recalled.

Dr. Renate Kimbrough, a member of the CDC research team, explained, "I was getting a hundred calls a day. I was trying to make studies that I hoped would help solve the problem. I could either work or I could return telephone calls. I chose to work."

By the end of the first week of August, Fraser and his team had added staff to answer phones and were getting on with the work at hand. One significant piece of good news—the number of new cases had begun to drop—seemed to mean that the epidemic was ending on its own. With the threat of additional deaths lessening, the team had time to carefully sort out and analyze the data they had collected.

A total of 182 people had become ill. Seventy-two of them were not Legionnaires, but had been in or near the Bellevue Stratford Hotel at the time of outbreak. Twenty-nine persons had died from lung complications. Those who were infected tended to be older males who smoked.

The first Legionnaire had gotten sick on July 23; then more and more had fallen ill each day, quickly reaching a peak of twenty-five per day on July 25. After that, fewer cases developed. This pattern told Fraser that all the sick were exposed at the same time and the same place. The infection had not been passed from person to person, because if that had happened more cases would have appeared as time went on.

Investigations had ruled out contaminated food, water, and other items in and around the hotel. Every person, place, and thing looked innocent. The same was true in the laboratories. In fact, the Legionnaires' illness did not seem to be caused by anything known to science.

Baffled, the team asked themselves again—what was it, and where had it come from?

Scientists and doctors did not know the answers to those questions, but the public thought it did. Every day the mail, newspapers, and television offered new solutions.

Some insisted poison was involved. A group of long-haired young people had picketed the Bellevue Stratford during the American Legion Convention, protesting past involvement in the Vietnam War.

Someone suggested that the "hippies" had slipped something into the hotel's water supply.

One of the Legionnaires claimed to have seen a glassy-eyed stranger in a blue suit in the hotel during the convention. He had supposedly carried a bag of some sort inside his jacket, with a tube running down his sleeve to his left hand which he pointed at the Legionnaires.

One letter writer suggested that the disease came from outer space. Another decided that it was the swine flu (a "killer" virus that posed a threat to the United States for a time).

The theories ranged from amusing to disturbing, but none of them checked out. As weeks and months passed, the CDC team continued to look for something they could weigh, measure, or photograph. Dr. Fraser expressed their frustration. "I despaired that we'd solve it," he confessed.

Then, in late December, a copy of the complete Legionnaire report came into the hands of Dr. Joseph McDade, a young microbiologist (a scientist who studies microorganisms such as bacteria). McDade worked in the Leprosy and Rickettsial Lab at the CDC.

McDade had previously eliminated rickettsias as a possible cause of Legion fever. But now it was Christmas vacation, and he was alone in the lab with some spare time. Out of curiosity, he scanned the report again. Right away, he noticed a fact he had missed before. Rickettsial infections, especially Q fever, had never been absolutely ruled out as the cause.

McDade grabbed a microscope and the Legionnaire slides. Back in August, when a quick identification of the disease had been high priority, he had looked at each slide for about five minutes. Now he spent thirty minutes on each.

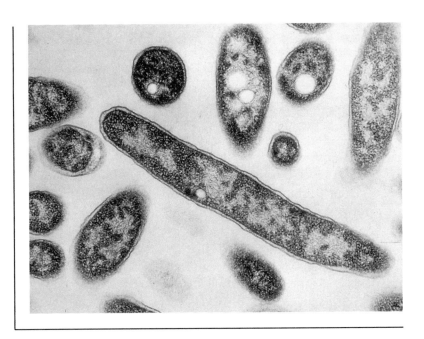

It took the determined sleuthing of doctors from the Centers for Disease Control to isolate and identify the killer strain of bacteria they called Legionella pneumophila.

Suddenly, he saw something unusual.

There, in the middle of a slide, was a cluster of red, sausage-shaped rods. McDade had never seen them, or anything like them, before. Excitedly, he called in his supervisor. Both men agreed that the rods were disease-causing microbes. But did they cause the Legionnaires' illness?

Using some of the carefully preserved infected tissue from the original tests, McDade began testing to find out. A week later, his results left no room for doubt. The rods were the culprits. Delightedly, McDade released his results to Fraser and the press.

It had taken six months, but the investigating team now had the answer to "what." The killer was a strain of bacteria (not rickettsias after all) that the researchers named *Legionella pneumophila*. It had been overlooked in earlier testing because it could grow only on a special growing medium called charcoal yeast extract agar, high in iron and the amino acid cysteine.

Where had it come from? Where had it laid hidden before attacking the Legionnaires.

McDade and Fraser could not be certain, but over time, they were able to make an educated guess. The bacteria was not new. Examining samples of infected blood and tissue saved from past cases, McDade linked the rods to at least two unsolved epidemics in 1965 and 1968. Later studies of *Legionella* showed that it had probably existed in soil and water from earliest times.

Although the scientists had no proof, they speculated that *Legionella* had drifted into the air-conditioning cooling towers on the roof of the hotel and began multiplying in the warm water there. The bacteria-infected water circulated through the hotel by way of the air-conditioning system. Some of it ran down the side of the building, reaching the street as a mist that infected anyone within a block of the hotel. But by the time the investigators checked the water, several weeks after the first cases of Legion fever were reported, conditions had changed and the bacteria had disappeared.

•••••

Most people are now content with the official explanation of the Bellevue Stratford mystery. The Legionnaires' epidemic was caused by bacteria carried in the air-cooling system of the hotel. The infection was not passed from person to person. It could be controlled with a common antibiotic, erythromycin.

But scientists are aware that *Legionella* can be found everywhere, from shower heads to mountain lakes. It strikes an estimated 50,000 Americans every year. Those most susceptible are old people who smoke, and persons with damaged immune systems.

The danger from *Legionella* has not passed. This once-mysterious bacterium is still an ominous threat today.

Chapter 2

The Great Imitator

When Jan Carlson, a successful lawyer in New York City, noticed a tiny bump on the back of her knee one summer weekend in 1985, she never dreamed that it was anything more than a mosquito bite, an irritation to be tolerated until it went away. After all, a bug bite or two was a small price to pay for the chance to spend a weekend at her summer home in the pretty Connecticut countryside.

By Sunday evening when Jan returned to the city, the bite had become a red rash. In addition, she ached all over and her temperature was 100.5°F (38.1°C). Guessing that the bite was the problem—perhaps it was infected—and not wanting to miss work the next day, Jan called her doctor that night.

The doctor was unconcerned and diagnosed Jan's illness as a virus. But several days—and several frustrating doctor's appointments—later, Jan felt worse. A throbbing headache kept her from sleeping. The rash had not subsided. She had missed work.

Then Jan received a call from a concerned relative who knew of her illness. He told Jan of an article he had just read about a disease passed through the bite of a deer tick, a small wingless insect that feeds on the blood of animals, including humans. Was Jan aware that the tick and the disease were widespread in the Connecticut area where her country home was located?

Jan protested that she would have noticed a tick on her body, and that her rash did not exactly match the description given in the article. However, the writer noted that not all Lyme disease rashes looked the same. And there was no denying the illness that showed no signs of going away. According to the article, if the disease was left untreated, the possible complications were frightening: heart problems, paralysis, and arthritis. Jan put in another call to her doctor, insisting on a second opinion.

The next morning, her pain even more intense, she met with a specialist. For him, one look was enough. Jan's symptoms were classic. He diagnosed her condition as Lyme disease.

Jan Carlson, and many Americans like her, knew little or nothing about Lyme disease in 1985. Polly Murray knew. Her life had never been the same since she had become one of the first victims of the disease two decades before.

Polly's struggle began in the 1960s in the New England town of Lyme, Connecticut, where she lived.

"I began having periodic flu-like illnesses, headaches, and odd rashes," she reported. "In 1967 the doctor thought I had rheumatic fever because of a painful, swollen knee."

Years passed, and Polly developed additional complaints—fever, stiff neck, painful, swollen joints.

She went to the doctor, who offered new diagnoses, but no treatment seemed effective over time.

Polly might have continued to put up with her mysterious troubles if they had not spread to her family. Beginning in the fall of 1974 and spanning a period of a year, Polly's husband and four children developed a variety of symptoms ranging from rashes and joint pain to severe headaches, fever, and facial paralysis. The family doctor seemed unable to get to the root of the problem. The symptoms seemed to come and go.

What was plaguing the Murrays? Polly had her own opinion. "I was convinced that everyone in the family had the same thing, but doctors kept looking at us independently. None could imagine that all our ills were related."

Being a strong-minded woman, she resolved to try and find the answer for herself. In spite of her continual illnesses, she began visiting medical libraries and reading anything that might shed light on the mystery. She talked to doctors. She questioned neighbors and friends, wondering if any of them had experienced the same symptoms.

Surprisingly, some had. One neighbor's child suffered from joint pain. A friend's teenager had rashes. A man complained of headaches and swollen knees.

The trouble was more widespread than Polly had expected. "I worried about what we all might be eating, or whether it was something in our well water, or whether it might be due to the nuclear plant nearby," she confessed.

Then, in the fall of 1975, Polly's twelve-year-old son, Todd, was diagnosed as having juvenile rheumatoid arthritis (JRA), a chronic and painful disease of the joints that affects children.

As Polly prepared to take him to a special clinic at the Yale University School of Medicine in New Haven, she was surprised to hear that a large number of children in the Lyme area had also been diagnosed with JRA. "It seemed . . . strange for so many children in our area, children living next door to each other, to have developed it," she reflected.

Polly first reported the unusual findings to her doctor, then to David Snydman, an official at the Connecticut State Health Department. Coincidentally, the department had just heard from another mother who reported the same thing. Health officials were planning a further investigation.

Not content to wait, Polly set to work, calling everyone she could find in her area who had been touched by JRA. Between November 1 and 21, she uncovered thirty-five cases. After sharing her findings with Dr. Allen Steere, a specialist at Yale, her suspicions were confirmed. The incidence of juvenile rheumatoid arthritis in the Lyme area was over *one hundred times* higher than in the general population.

The mystery was not yet solved, but Polly was encouraged. Both Dr. Snydman and Dr. Steere agreed to investigate. It was a step in the right direction.

Steere and Snydman had both worked for a time at the Centers for Disease Control (CDC) in Atlanta, Georgia. Like all good CDC investigators, they had been trained to respond quickly to reports of unusual outbreaks of disease. They eagerly took over where Polly Murray left off, convinced that they were on the trail of a previously unknown disease, which they called Lyme arthritis.

Almost immediately, they realized that the investigation would be more complicated than they had expected. A growing number of patients described an array of problems that ranged from rashes to irregular heartbeats. Obviously the disease was something more than arthritis.

Convinced, as Polly Murray had been, that there was some common cause of the epidemic, Steere and Snydman began looking for things the victims might have in common. "We checked them all. Food, water, drugs, immunizations, other diseases, pets—you name it."

Two significant clues came to light. First, victims usually experienced their initial symptoms—most typically a red "bull's-eye" rash—in late spring or summer. Next, all of the victims lived in or near heavily wooded areas. Past experience with other diseases led the men to believe that they were looking for a disease-causing organism carried by an insect, one that lived on vegetation and was active in the spring. In 1978 they narrowed the field of suspects to the deer tick (also known as the bear tick in the Midwest), *Ixodes dammini*. A victim happened to notice one of the tiny creatures— normally smaller than the head of a pin—and brought it in for inspection.

The carrier appeared to have been identified, but the cause—whether bacterium, virus, or something else—promised to be more difficult to isolate.

By now, scientists at the CDC and other research institutions had joined in the search. Failing to discover suspicious bacteria in samples of patients' blood, the scientists first theorized that the cause might be a virus. They looked unsuccessfully for more than two hundred viruses in victims' blood before hearing that European doctors had been moderately successful in treating the disease with penicillin, an antibiotic.

Deer ticks, normally the size of pinheads, appear magnified here on a fingertip. Lurking on grass blades and leaves, these tiny creatures can pass on the debilitating, lifelong effects of Lyme disease with one painless bite.

This was progress. If the organism responded to penicillin treatment, it was probably not a virus. (Penicillin effectively kills many bacteria, but not viruses.) American researchers quickly changed their emphasis. In 1982, Willy Burgdorfer, a scientist at the National Institute of Allergy and Infectious Diseases in Hamilton, Montana, triumphantly announced the isolation of the agent of the disease, a spirochete bacterium later named *Borrelia burgdorferi*.

Further searches through medical literature seemed to prove that the organism was not new after all. Similar illnesses had been reported in the past in Europe, including one Swedish case in 1910 that linked the disease to a tick bite.

• • • • •

Lyme disease is no longer an unnamed mystery, yet in many ways, it remains a puzzle to victims and doctors alike. Like a master of disguise that changes its appearance at will, it can be a mild illness to some, a crippler to others. In a few cases, it has been fatal.

Neither Jan Carlson nor the Murray family experienced the full range of its devastation. Nicknamed "the great imitator," it mimics a wide variety of diseases, among them arthritis, mononucleosis, strep throat, the flu, and multiple sclerosis. Complications, which are common, range from seizures and hearing loss to mood swings and birth defects.

Lyme disease is difficult to diagnose. A blood test that reveals antibodies to the disease is available but considered unreliable by some doctors. And although the disease can be controlled or eliminated with early antibiotic treatment, there are no guarantees. Jan Carlson continued to feel sharp pain in her hips after the first ten-day course of medication. Only when her doctor, a Lyme disease specialist, prescribed a double dose of a different antibiotic did her condition improve. Even then, tingling in her left hand led her to wonder if there were more problems ahead.

Lyme disease continues to be a threat in the United States, especially the Northeast, although a new vaccine now offers the promise of future protection. (A vaccine is already available for dogs and cats.)

For people like Polly Murray who did not get early treatment, though, there is little hope of a complete cure. Still, these courageous individuals work to spread the word about Lyme disease.

Until it is defeated, they are convinced that the public's best defense is to know the enemy they are fighting.

Chapter 3

The Vampire Virus

Marybelle Tilson was unconscious and near death when she entered Parkland City–County Hospital in Dallas, Texas, on October 30, 1951.

The forty-three-year-old homemaker's illness had begun innocently enough with flulike symptoms. After several days, her fever skyrocketed to over 103°F (39.4°C), and the family doctor admitted her to a local hospital in her West Texas hometown. When Marybelle became panic-stricken, and then lost the ability to swallow, speak, or move her left arm, she was transferred to Parkland, a larger, better-equipped facility in Dallas.

In Parkland's intensive care unit, an attending physician quickly diagnosed Marybelle's illness as bulbar poliomyelitis, a severe form of polio. Epidemics of polio were common at that time, and Marybelle had many of the symptoms. For four days, doctors fought to break the deadly grip of the disease, but in the end, every effort failed. Marybelle died.

Something about his patient's symptoms, perhaps the report of her unexplained terror, troubled Marybelle's doctor. With Hank Tilson's consent, an autopsy (examination of the body to determine cause of death) was performed. When the report came back, it included astonishing news: "encephalomyelitis with demonstrable Negri bodies in central motor neurons . . ."

Negri bodies! The words flashed like a red light before the doctor's eyes. Their presence instantly changed the diagnosis. Marybelle had not died of polio. She had died of rabies.

A case of human rabies was very rare, but the Parkland doctor knew about the disease. Caused by a virus (a microscopic infective agent that multiplies only in connection with living cells), rabies is passed to the victim through contaminated saliva during a bite. The virus then grows and reproduces in nerve tissue such as the brain and spinal cord. Its identifying marks are Negri bodies, distinctive clusters of cells left in the victim's brain.

The doctor guessed that Marybelle had probably not been alarmed by her early symptoms—a scratchy throat, dull headache, and occasional nausea. She might have worried a little when her left arm began to tingle and ache, but by that time even the best treatment would have been too late. The virus had already become entrenched in her system. Marybelle's fate had been determined when she had been bitten by an animal— the doctor was certain that she had been bitten—and failed to get immediate help.

After breaking the news to her husband, the doctor asked him to think carefully over the last month or two. Rabies often had a long and variable incubation time (the period between the time disease organisms enter the victim and the first appearance of symptoms). Could Mr. Tilson think of a time recently when his wife had received an animal bite?

Hank Tilson didn't have to think. He knew. His wife had been attacked by a bat on October 9. She had come across it lying in the road near their house. When she bent over to take a look, the animal had sprung at her and nipped her arm before flying away.

The doctor frowned. It sounded like the event they were looking for. Unfortunately, it had to be a coincidence. Bat rabies was a disease found only in vampire bats in South America and Mexico. Years of research had proven that vampire bats never traveled north into the United States.

Hank insisted, but the doctor remained firm. There must have been another bite from another animal. A few cases of rabies cropped up in dogs, cats, and skunks every year. That was the most reasonable explanation. Either Mr. Tilson had forgotten the incident, or his wife had neglected to tell him.

The doctor closed the case, but the question remained unanswered. How had Marybelle Tilson contracted rabies? Hank Tilson was not the kind of man to argue. He could only scratch his head and wonder.

The case might have been forgotten, if not for Donald Bright and Flora Robbins.

Donald Bright was the seven-year-old son of a ranch hand living near Tampa, Florida. On the morning of June 23, 1953, the boy was playing in his yard. Suddenly, without warning, a bat flew out of the bushes. It swooped at Donald a couple of times, then attached itself to his clothes and fiercely bit him on the chest.

*While hoary bats are not the only animals to carry rabies,
they may be the scariest. Bats have long had an undeserved
reputation for unprovoked attacks on humans.*

Screaming, Donald ran to his parents, who tore the animal off and threw it to the ground. While Mrs. Bright hustled her bleeding son into the house, Mr. Bright killed the bat.

The owner of the ranch learned of the extraordinary episode later that day. Having heard tales of vampire bat rabies in Mexico, he insisted that the Brights take their son and the bat into town for an examination.

Presented with a dead bat, the Brights' doctor notified the Florida State Health Department, which was responsible for preventing and controlling disease within the state. The bat was examined. It was a Florida yellow, an insect-eater, not a blood-loving vampire. In spite of that, the evidence was clear. It had attacked a human being, and its brain contained Negri bodies, typical of rabies.

Three months later in Boiling Springs, Pennsylvania, thirty-four-year-old Flora Robbins was standing at the edge of a lake, watching her husband feed ducks. All of a sudden, a heavy object struck her arm and hung there, squirming and scratching. With a shriek, she grabbed whatever it was and threw it against a nearby fence.

Mr. Robbins, an amateur naturalist, heard the commotion and ran to help. One look told him the object was a bat. Thinking quickly, he trapped it in a pail, then took his wife and the animal to the doctor.

By the next morning the bat had died. Mrs. Robbins's doctor prudently notified the Pennsylvania Department of Health, and the animal's body was sent in for examination. Again, it was not a vampire, but an insect-loving hoary bat. Positive evidence of rabies was found.

Bat rabies in the United States! The discovery stunned doctors and public health authorities. Would there be other cases? Had millions of once harmless creatures now turned into an unpredictable menace, ready to attack anyone, anywhere?

In the face of a possible epidemic, the health department notified the Centers for Disease Control (CDC), in Atlanta, Georgia. While the CDC began its investigation, the doctors treating Donald Bright and Flora Robbins acted quickly to protect their patients from the disease.

Their only option at that time was the "Pasteur treatment," a series of up to fourteen painful injections almost identical to those Louis Pasteur had used on his first patient, Joseph Meister, in 1885. Nine-year-old Joseph had been attacked and repeatedly bitten by a rabid dog.

Before Pasteur's time, treatment of rabies had been as varied as it was unsuccessful. Early remedies ranged from searing the wound with a red-hot iron to drinking a mixture of thirty herbal ingredients (including poppy tears, Illyrian iris, Gallic nard, white pepper, male frankincense, and turpentine, mixed with honey and dissolved in a tumbler of wine).

Pasteur's vaccine, a weakened strain of the virus that produced protective antibodies in the victim, was the first treatment reliable enough to be called a "cure." It saved Joseph Meister then, and it saved Donald Bright and Flora Robbins in 1953.

Within months, their cases were added to Joseph's in the medical books. In all the excitement, Marybelle Tilson's case lay hidden in the past. The first apparent incidents of bat rabies in the United States had been logged. The future of the disease was of top importance to health officials now.

The problem was too widespread and too time-consuming for one scientist or team of scientists to

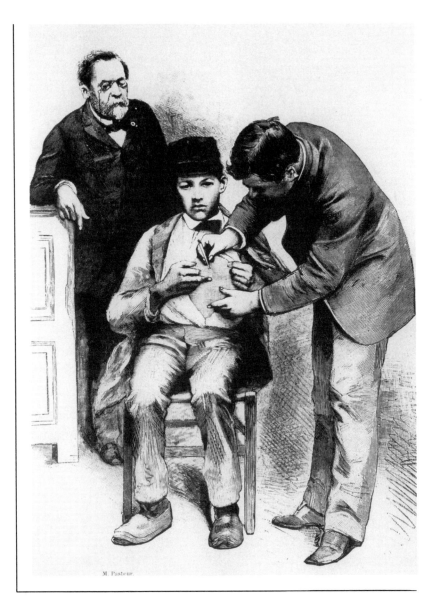

M. Pasteur.

In a Harper's Weekly *illustration that appeared in 1885, Louis Pasteur observes a young boy receiving a rabies-preventative inoculation.*

tackle alone. Researchers in state health departments across the country supported the CDC's efforts, trapping and studying bats, trying to find the answers to important questions. How many bats were infected? Was an epidemic of human rabies from bats on the way?

The first answers seemed to indicate horrifying possibilities. On February 1, 1956, a headline in the *Santa Fe New Mexican* screamed, "Carlsbad Cave Bats Infected With Rabies." The article revealed that, while following up an incident involving dead and dying bats on the floor of the famous caverns, the New Mexico State Department of Public Health discovered that more than half of the dead bats carried the rabies virus.

The news spread across the country like wildfire. Further studies revealed the alarming fact that, although the Carlsbad bats had died of the disease, bats in other areas seemed able to carry rabies and pass it along while remaining healthy. The CDC issued a report citing bats as a major source of danger from the disease. It seemed possible that the threat of rabid bat attacks might grow until it hung over the future like a black cloud.

Time and experience proved the threat to be less than experts feared. Nevertheless, bat rabies could no longer be considered "the vampire virus," confined to blood-loving bats in tropical regions of the world. In the years that followed, rabies-carrying bats were reported in every state but Alaska and Hawaii. Of seven cases of human rabies that occurred in the United States between 1980 and 1991, five were caused by bats.

The disease, however, is not confined to bats. Incidents of rabies have risen in other wild animals in the recent past. New York State listed 225 cases of reported animal rabies in 1991, as compared with 54 in 1989. Animals that posed the greatest danger included red foxes, skunks, and raccoons. Raccoons are especially dangerous because they fearlessly wander into neighborhoods looking for food. Rabid raccoons have been known to attack without provocation, sometimes biting dogs and cats, which in turn can pass the disease to their owners.

Only the development of a new vaccine makes the news less frightening. People bitten by suspected rabid animals now face only five injections into the upper arm or back rather than fourteen shots into the abdomen as required before. And for persons at highest risk— veterinarians and cave explorers—a vaccine, to be taken before exposure, is also available.

· · · · ·

As bat rabies became a fact of life in the United States, a doctor involved in Marybelle Tilson's case remembered the unhappy affair, and the husband who had stubbornly insisted that a bat had been involved.

Referring to the files, the doctor checked the date. It had been 1951, two years before the Florida and Pennsylvania incidents. The medical community had been ignorant of the facts then.

History now stands corrected. The Tilson case has replaced Donald Bright's as the first occurrence of bat rabies in the United States. Marybelle's illness was tragic and probably unnecessary, but her death is a mystery no longer.

Chapter
4

A Merciless Enemy

As a doctor at the University of California at Los Angeles School of Medicine, Michael Gottlieb regularly came in contact with rare and remarkable cases. Few health problems had the power to surprise him anymore.

Still, he was puzzled when he examined Ken Darby one January day in 1981. Darby had been admitted to the hospital for treatment of candidiasis, or thrush, a fungal infection characterized by soreness and white patches in the mouth and throat.

The doctor usually saw candidiasis in patients with damaged or immature immune systems, especially newborn babies and people receiving chemotherapy. Darby was thirty-one years old and claimed to be in good health—except for his throat. It was so sore and swollen that he could barely swallow or breathe.

Gottlieb performed a few routine blood tests on his patient. The results clearly showed a startling reason for Darby's condition. His blood contained very few T-helper cells (cells that assist in the production of antibodies and help fight infection). Without them, Darby was at great risk to catch almost any disease that came his way.

Still, the man seemed healthy enough. For the time being, Gottlieb adopted a "wait and see" approach, gave his patient the appropriate treatment for candidiasis, and sent him home.

A few weeks later, Darby was back, this time suffering from a form of pneumonia, *Pneumocystis carinii*, usually found only in patients with damaged immune systems. He complained of being tired. Further tests revealed that he also had anemia (low numbers of oxygen-carrying cells in the blood, causing a feeling of weakness or tiredness).

In the coming weeks, doctors put forth their best efforts to treat Darby's problems, but with no success. His health went from bad to worse, and he died a short time later, the cause of his sudden ill health still a mystery.

Later that spring, Dr. Gottlieb was again surprised when another young man, Jerry Brantley, entered the hospital with the same disturbing symptoms as Darby—candidiasis and an abnormally low number of T-helper cells in his blood. Brantley had also lost a significant amount of weight and had respiratory and digestive problems. Tests of his lungs revealed that he, too, suffered from *Pneumocystis carinii* pneumonia.

Brantley's personal doctor, Joel Weisman, was quick to point out that he had recently seen other patients—all young male homosexuals—with similar symptoms. They had also complained of fever and swollen lymph glands (part of the body's immune system). Jerry Brantley and the other men seemed unable to recover from their complaints, in spite of proper treatment.

Dr. Gottlieb, anxious to see if anyone else had seen this rather unusual condition, put in a call to the Los Angeles County Department of Public Health. The doctor there searched his records and turned up only one reported case of *Pneumocystis carinii* pneumonia. After checking with neighboring health departments, he discovered another.

By May 1981, the number stood at five, and Gottlieb called the Centers for Disease Control (CDC) in Atlanta, Georgia, to alert them to the epidemic storm clouds that he feared were looming on the horizon. The number of cases was small, and the CDC could not even be sure that Gottlieb was reporting a contagious disease. Still, they promised to investigate the situation. Dr. James Curran, then chief of the Venereal Disease branch, was put in charge.

At about the same time, a slightly different problem arose in the eastern part of the United States. As early as the fall of 1979, Linda Laubenstein, a doctor at New York University Medical Center, came across a case of Kaposi's sarcoma, a rare form of cancer usually found in older men of Jewish or Mediterranean descent. Her patient did not fit the pattern. He was young and neither Mediterranean nor Jewish.

Soon after, an associate notified Dr. Laubenstein of a similar case of Kaposi's sarcoma at a Brooklyn medical center. By March 1981, at least eight cases had been identified, all of them in young male homosexuals. As a rule the cancer spread slowly, but by March, four of these eight were already dead.

Dr. Curran of the CDC, investigating the Los Angeles cases, also took an interest in those in New York. The link between the two was the report of at least one patient in San Francisco who had both Kaposi's sarcoma and *Pneumocystis carinii* pneumonia.

A CDC report, dated July 3, 1981, set out the early findings. Twenty-six young homosexual men (twenty in New York and six in California) had been diagnosed with Kaposi's sarcoma. At least four also suffered from *Pneumocystis carinii* pneumonia. All showed evidence of damaged immune systems.

It seemed clear to Curran and other researchers that the cancer and pneumonia were simply expressions of a more complex problem—the unexplained breakdown of the immune system that normally protected these men from disease. With little or no protection, their bodies had been unable to defend themselves.

The CDC's advice to doctors was straightforward and gave no clue to the frustration and controversy that would follow: "Physicians should be alert for Kaposi's sarcoma, *Pneumocystis carinii* pneumonia, and other . . . infections associated with immunosuppression in homosexual men."

As word of the strange new phenomenon began to spread within the medical community, the CDC set up two criteria to define it. First, infections had to be related to a breakdown of the T-helper cells in the immune system. Second, there had to be no other cause for the immune deficiency, such as drugs used for cancer therapy or after organ transplants.

The CDC directed doctors to look for certain specific diseases in addition to the cancer and pneumonia that seemed to appear in association with the syndrome: primary lymphoma of the central nervous system (a type of brain cancer), toxoplasmosis (an infection that attacks the heart, eyes, and central nervous system), and candidiasis, to name a few.

Questions abounded. Was the immune system shutdown caused by some genetic weakness? Could it be due to something in the homosexual life-style? Was an organism of some kind responsible? If so, was it contagious, and how was it passed?

The number of cases, and deaths, kept climbing. By August 28, 1981, just three months after its first tally of 5 cases, the CDC's total stood at 108. Forty percent of those people were already dead at the time of the report.

With no time to be lost, researchers from the Centers for Disease Control, the National Institutes of Health, the World Health Organization, and the Pasteur Institute in France (the mysterious syndrome had appeared in Europe as well) began working to find answers.

The CDC, involved from the beginning, attacked the problem from two different directions. After gathering samples of tissue and fluids from the sick men, scientists began a thorough search for any organism or chemical substance that might lead to the destruction of T-helper cells. At the same time, field investigators questioned the infected men and their doctors for clues that might explain the cause of the mysterious "disease" that would soon be known as AIDS (Acquired Immune Deficiency Syndrome).

Initial laboratory research proved frustrating. Researchers pinpointed any number of bacteria and viruses under their microscopes. All seemed to be

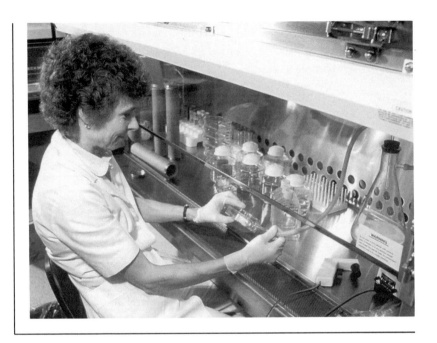

A CDC lab worker performs a test using samples of dried blood. Tests such as this can be used to detect antibodies to viruses and, with luck, to identify them.

opportunistic infections that were present because of the weakened or deficient immune systems. No known agent—viral, bacterial, or fungal—that might be responsible for the immune system breakdown could be identified.

Field work proved more valuable. Crisscrossing the United States, the CDC team interviewed as many physicians and patients as they could locate. They eliminated any number of factors such as food, clothing, and environment that the patients might have shared and that might have caused the problem. Of special interest were "poppers" (amyl and butyl nitrate), illegal drugs used by the majority of the young men. But these, too, were ruled out.

What was left was a single common denominator—all the patients were homosexuals who had been involved with many different partners. One group of AIDS patients in Los Angeles reported a more or less regular exchange of partners within the group. Another patient, in New York, had been the partner of four infected men in the Los Angeles group, as well as with four others in the infected New York group. Many of the men also admitted that they had been repeatedly infected with sexually transmitted diseases such as gonorrhea, syphilis, and genital herpes.

The beginning of 1982 brought tragic new developments. The number of people with AIDS began to climb exponentially, with ten new cases being reported each week. And from San Francisco to New York, a new group began to appear, people like Wendy Miller who had had a blood transfusion in the past and Sheila Roseman, an intravenous drug abuser. Others at risk included hemophiliacs ("bleeders" who use clotting factors from donated blood to treat their disease) and Haitian refugees (incidence of AIDS is high in this Caribbean nation).

In the face of the growing tragedy, there was one encouraging factor. Researchers were now virtually certain that they were looking for some organism that could be passed from person to person in an exchange of body fluids. The organism was transferred on contaminated needles shared by drug addicts, in blood from infected donors, in semen during sexual activity.

Hearing the news that AIDS was contagious, the public panicked. Health officials emphasized that certain groups were most at risk: homosexuals, Haitians, drug addicts, prostitutes, and hemophiliacs. Still, the disease was fatal, and no one knew the full extent of the danger involved. If AIDS was passed in body fluids, were saliva and tears also contagious? Were families and friends of persons with AIDS in grave danger?

Scientists hastened to look for answers to those questions. (There had been no proven cases of AIDS passed by saliva or tears, and family members did not appear to be at exceptional risk.) Meanwhile, two research groups—one American, one French— redoubled their efforts to isolate and identify the disease-causing organism.

Dr. Robert Gallo of the National Cancer Institute in Bethesda, Maryland, headed the American team. Gallo had recently discovered the first cancer-causing retrovirus in humans. (Retro means "backward"; the retrovirus invades a cell and then reverses the usual process by which the cell copies its genetic code. Retroviruses are particularly lethal, because the virus cannot be killed without also killing the infected cell.) He reasoned that his team might be looking for a new but similar retrovirus in the AIDS cases, especially since all other viruses had been eliminated as possibilities. Gallo began his search with the T-helper cells. They were the first to come under attack; they might hold the key to the puzzle.

Dr. Luc Montagnier, head of the French research team at the Pasteur Institute in Paris, reasoned in much the same way as Gallo. Using similar methods, he too grew and experimented with T-cells in the institute's laboratory.

In May 1983, Montagnier and his team announced the isolation of what they *thought* was the retrovirus

Dr. Luc Montagnier of the Pasteur Institute in Paris, speaking at the VII International Conference on AIDS in 1991.

that caused AIDS, naming it LAV (lymphadenopathy-associated virus). In the spring of 1984, Gallo's announcement was more confident. He claimed his team had definitely isolated the retrovirus that caused AIDS. They dubbed it HTLV-III (human T-cell leukemia virus, Type III).

The two viruses proved to have only minor variations and were subsequently treated as one, renamed HIV (human immunodeficiency virus). News of the discovery of the cause of AIDS was reported worldwide. Unhappily, the triumphant event was marred by controversy. Both teams insisted that they were the first to have achieved the historic breakthrough. Montagnier suggested that Gallo had simply re-isolated a sample of LAV sent to him from the Pasteur Institute earlier that year. Gallo denied the possibility, but could not disprove the suspicions.

The controversy continued. In 1992, a panel from the National Institutes of Health ruled out unethical behavior on Gallo's part. Later that year, however, a Health and Human Services investigation found him guilty of scientific misconduct. They judged that he had deliberately falsified data in his 1984 report, thereby casting doubt on Montagnier's work.

Gallo again contested the findings, but some speculated that the United States government might have to turn over to the French the millions of dollars in profit it had earned from the AIDS antibody test kit it patented earlier.

• • • • •

In the years since young men like Ken Darby and Jerry Brantley began to die, many questions about AIDS have been answered. Experts can say with confidence that HIV is passed by exchange of infected body fluids, never by casual contact such as hugging or holding hands. They know that AIDS infects men, women, and children, and that, through education and responsible behavior, it can be controlled and prevented.

Researchers have learned more about the virus itself. They have tracked the way the human body reacts to HIV. They have discovered medicines that can prolong the life of people with AIDS. Promising developments in vaccine research emphasize the fact that more answers are on the way.

AIDS has been a merciless opponent, but the medical detectives continue to fight. The enemy remains to be beaten.

Chapter 5

What's Wrong with Johnny?

When Johnny Cavana and his mother entered Dr. Robert Lanford's office on the afternoon of October 4, 1961, the receptionist took one look and rushed to get the doctor. She knew an emergency when she saw one, and Johnny was a real emergency.

Dr. Lanford came on the run and carried the eight-year-old into an examining room. Johnny was obviously sick, and getting sicker by the minute. He was clutching his stomach and vomiting. His skin was gray. His breathing was irregular. His face and arms twitched. A few minutes later, he began to lose consciousness.

From some of the symptoms—vomiting, abnormal breathing, coma—Dr. Lanford guessed that Johnny might have diabetes (a disorder in which the body cannot use sugar normally, causing a buildup of dangerous amounts of sugar in the blood). If that condition was left untreated, he could easily die.

Still, the doctor hesitated. Johnny was also experiencing severe abdominal pain, and that was not typical of diabetes. Wisely, Dr. Lanford put in a quick call for help to noted Fresno pediatrician Dr. John Conrad, Jr.

Dr. Conrad listened and agreed that treatment was urgent. He suggested that Johnny be rushed to Valley Children's Hospital, where he met the boy a short time later.

If anything, Johnny's condition was worse than Dr. Lanford had described it. His pulse was racing. He was salivating. His temperature was up. While being examined, he cried out twice from stomach pain. Dr. Conrad also noted that the pupils of the boy's eyes were contracted as small as pinpoints.

It was an unusual combination of symptoms, but the doctor thought of two conditions that could explain them.

The first was shigellosis (caused by the *Shigella* bacteria), an infection involving serious inflammation of the lining of the intestine. Johnny had many of the symptoms.

The second possibility, pesticide poisoning, seemed more likely to Dr. Conrad. The variety of symptoms, especially the abdominal pain, contracted pupils, and salivation, were typical of the disorder. In addition, the records stated that the Cavanas lived on the outskirts of town, surrounded by fields. Fresno County, California, was an important agricultural area where treating crops with poisonous chemicals was an everyday occurrence at certain times of the year. Mrs. Cavana had also mentioned that Johnny had seen spraying equipment and a crop-dusting plane while waiting for the bus that morning.

Workers using spraying equipment to apply pesticides wear protective gear, but no protection is available to innocent people who may happen to be in the area.

Even before a laboratory test ruled out shigellosis, Dr. Conrad felt certain enough of his diagnosis of pesticide poisoning to start treatment.

He began by ordering intravenous fluids (fluids injected slowly into a vein) to replace those Johnny had lost. Then he prescribed a series of atropine injections. Atropine, a drug made from the deadly nightshade plant, would counteract the symptoms if poisoning was indeed the cause.

By late evening, Dr. Conrad brought Mrs. Cavana the good news. The laboratory at Fresno's Poison Control Center had confirmed the diagnosis of chemical poisoning, and Johnny was improving. His pupils were returning to normal size. He was alert; his temperature and heartbeat had returned to normal.

The doctor was satisfied that with time and care, Johnny would soon be back to normal. The incident had been unusual but easily explained. The case was as good as over.

The first glimmer of trouble came a few days later. Dr. Conrad learned that the spraying rigs Johnny had reported seeing had, in fact, *not* been applying pesticides that day.

The doctor was puzzled but reminded himself that spraying was common in the area. Johnny might have been exposed at a different time and not even noticed. Besides, the case was closed. The boy was back to normal. He had recovered at home and was eager to go back to school.

Dr. Conrad gave him the okay one afternoon the following week. After that short appointment, Johnny waved good-bye, and the doctor made preparations for his next appointment.

Half an hour later, real trouble struck.

The doctor was in the middle of an examination when his receptionist broke into the room. Mrs. Cavana was back, and she was almost hysterical! Johnny was out in the car. He was sick again. Could the doctor come quickly?

Dr. Conrad raced to the parking lot. There he found Johnny, pale and clammy and breathing fast.

Thinking quickly, the doctor slid into the front seat and directed Mrs. Cavana to drive to the hospital a block away. While she drove, she gasped out the story.

Johnny had been fine as they pulled out of the doctor's parking lot. He had seemed fine all the way home. Then, without warning, he became terribly sick. She had immediately turned around and driven back to town.

Dr. Conrad looked down at the limp little boy twitching in his arms. This attack was worse than the last, but the symptoms were the same. Johnny had been poisoned again.

Where had the poison come from? There had been no contact with spraying rigs, no outside poisons. The question was a matter of life and death, and Dr. Conrad had to admit he hadn't a clue to the answer.

He had little time to worry about that, however. Treating Johnny with atropine and fluids did not work as well this time. Dr. Conrad was forced to turn to a drug that was specific for chemical poisoning: pralidoxime chloride, or PAM for short. If it worked quickly, there was hope that Johnny's life could be saved.

For the next three hours, Mrs. Cavana and the doctor hovered over the boy. Then, slowly, the drug began to defeat the poison. The symptoms lessened. By morning, Johnny was out of immediate danger.

Now Dr. Conrad had time to think about the source of the poison. Johnny had been fine when he left home that afternoon. He had only been in the car and in the doctor's office. Somewhere, during that short time, he had come in contact with the poison again.

Finding the answer could take days of work. The doctor knew that he did not have the time to take on this part of the puzzle. He promptly put in a call to the Fresno County Health Department, notifying them of the poisoning and asking them to follow up on the case.

R.E. Bergstrom and Tiyo Yamaguchi, both from the Division of Environmental Health at the Fresno County Health Department, took over the investigation. While Johnny recovered, the two men visited the Cavana home, looking for clues.

The inside of the car was clear. The garage was free of garden sprays and insect bombs. Nothing inside the house looked suspicious.

Then they came to Johnny's clothes. As Mrs. Cavana showed the investigators her son's underwear and socks, pants and shirts, she mentioned five pairs of winter jeans she had recently purchased from the salvage depot of a trucking company in town. They had been a real bargain. Johnny had only worn them twice.

The men looked interested. Which days had he worn them?

Mrs. Cavana thought. It was the day he had come home sick from school, and the day he returned to Dr. Conrad for his final checkup.

Bergstrom and Yamaguchi smiled at each other. They had found the source of the poison. It had almost been too easy!

With Mrs. Cavana's permission, they carefully wrapped up the jeans and took them for testing to the State Department of Public Health. Researchers there raised colonies of mosquitoes for experimental purposes. The investigators placed the jeans into one of the insects' containers and sat back to watch.

Within fifteen minutes, every mosquito was dead. Five minutes after that, mosquitoes in a closed container 20 feet (6 meters) away started dying as well. There could be no doubt that the jeans had been contaminated with a highly toxic pesticide.

Leaving the identification of the poison to others (it was soon identified as Phosdrin, an organophosphate pesticide), Bergstrom and Yamaguchi began searching for any additional pairs of jeans that might have been sold at the salvage depot.

At about the same time, Dr. Conrad received a disturbing call from one of his medical students, a young resident at Fresno General Hospital.

The resident, Dr. Merritt Warren, had been on duty when an eight-year-old boy named Bobby Munson had been admitted to the hospital. After seeing the boy, Dr. Warren remembered Dr. Conrad's description of Johnny Cavana.

Bobby Munson's symptoms appeared suspiciously similar to Johnny's—irregular breathing, muscular twitches, abdominal cramps, vomiting, and pinpoint pupils. Although the family doctor had diagnosed the trouble as rheumatic fever, Dr. Warren guessed that Bobby's problem was another case of poisoned jeans.

The resident's guess proved correct. Investigation proved that Bobby Munson's jeans had come from the same salvage depot as Johnny's. The boy had worn them the day he got sick.

The case was no longer a single poisoning incident. It was a potential epidemic, and Bergstrom and Yamaguchi decided the public must be alerted. While Bobby and Johnny were recovering, the Health Department issued a news bulletin.

"County Warns Salvage Jeans Contain Poison," the front-page newspaper article announced. The jeans were dangerous, even deadly. Anyone thinking they had a suspicious pair were directed to bring them to the Health Department immediately.

Within days, a representative of a children's institution, as well as several concerned parents, turned in over two dozen pairs of jeans. Many tested positive for Phosdrin. When asked, all but one set of parents admitted that their sons had been seriously ill recently. Symptoms had been identical to Johnny's. Only luck and good medical care had saved their lives.

Weeks after Johnny's illness, Dr. Conrad, Bergstrom, and Yamaguchi learned the complete history of the poisoned jeans from a report filed by the State Public Utilities Commission (at that time, the agency responsible for investigating trucking violations). Manufactured at a plant south of Fresno and destined for a Los Angeles department store, the jeans had been shipped in a truck that also carried seventy-two cans of Phosdrin concentrate.

Somewhere on the journey, one of the cans had been punctured. At the department store, a shipping clerk noted a dark stain on the paper wrapped around the garments and rejected sixteen pairs of the jeans. They were eventually returned to the trucking company in Fresno. By then the stain had disappeared, and the jeans were put on sale at the company's salvage depot store. They looked as good as new.

Transporting hazardous material without taking special precautions was (and is) against the law in California. So is failing to report the damaged container to the proper authorities. After an investigation, the trucking company was found guilty and given the maximum fine—five thousand dollars.

With the mystery solved, one question nagged at Bergstrom and Yamaguchi. Out of all the children wearing the suspect jeans, only five had gotten sick. Why had the others not fallen victim to the poison?

The answer was as simple as soap and water. Mothers of the sick boys had allowed their sons to wear the new jeans just as they came from the store.

The other mother and the children's institution? They had been more careful. They had washed the jeans before they were worn.

• • • • •

At the time of the poisoned jeans incident, no one knew what long-term effects (if any) pesticide poisoning had on the human body. But a growing number of farmers and their employees had reported reactions similar to Johnny's after being accidentally sprayed with pesticides in the fields. Researchers began studying the problem.

Reports now establish the fact that even one incident of organophosphate poisoning in adults is enough to cause noticeable disturbances in speech, memory, and coordination years later. Experts have also proven that exposure to pesticides may cause cancer and birth defects. Because Johnny and the other boys were children, they were even more likely to experience physical problems sometime during their lifetimes.

At great risk are the thousands of field workers (and their children) who are still exposed almost daily to pesticides. Even "weekend gardeners," who use lawn and garden products in their yards, may face some danger.

Until health officials push for changes that will reduce the hazards, episodes similar to Johnny's are likely to continue. The case of the poisoned blue jeans must be remembered for the deadly warning that it carried.

Chapter
6

Death in
The Desert

The American Southwest, with its blazing sun and wide open spaces, seems an unlikely place for an outbreak of deadly disease. Epidemics have traditionally favored crowded conditions associated with the nation's inner cities. Yet, mysterious death has struck the desert more than once over time. One such case began in May 1981, in the small town of Cuba, New Mexico.

Twenty-eight-year-old Jimmy Bistie had a sore throat. Just trying to swallow brought tears to his eyes. Jimmy, a Navajo, had consulted several chanters, or medicine men, about his problem. No one had been able to help. With a throbbing head and aching muscles, he then turned to the Cuba Health Center as a last resort.

The physician's assistant who examined Jimmy was not overly concerned. Diagnosing the illness as a bad case of strep throat, he gave Jimmy penicillin and aspirin and sent him home with orders to rest.

But Jimmy's condition went from bad to worse in spite of the medication. His temperature shot up. A deep, persistent cough tore at his chest and made his head throb harder than ever. He had trouble getting his breath. Alarmed, he began to notice flecks of blood in his handkerchief after each coughing attack.

Convinced that "white man's medicine" would never cure her son, Jimmy's mother insisted that he visit another chanter. With his brother driving, Jimmy and his mother and sister set off to find a medicine man who lived on the Navajo Reservation in the northwestern part of the state.

Hours later, the long trip over the hot, dry hills ended in failure. The medicine man could not be found. Jimmy was now burning with fever, and the coughing was making it almost impossible for him to breathe. Badly frightened, his family rushed him south to the Gallup Indian Medical Center.

Jimmy was carried into the emergency room, where Dr. Molly Ettenger and her staff began working to save his life. Within minutes, however, Jimmy lost consciousness, then his heart stopped beating. While a nurse gave him mouth-to-mouth resuscitation, he was hooked to a respirator that helped him breathe. For another day, he held on to life. Then, the end came.

What had killed Jimmy Bistie?

The technicians in the Gallup lab were the first to find the answer. After examining samples of fluid from Jimmy's lungs, they hurried to telephone Dr. Ettenger. Black Death had struck in New Mexico. Jimmy Bistie had died of plague.

To most Americans, the word "plague" brings images of an ancient epidemic, as far removed from modern life as gloomy castles and knights in armor. But in

In this miniature taken from the fourteenth-century Toggenburg Bible, two plague victims receive the last rites from a priest.

the late Middle Ages, plague was an all-too-real threat to Europeans. Between the fourteenth and seventeenth centuries, almost half the population of that continent was wiped out by the Black Death, so named because of blood spots under the skin that turned black.

In 1894, Dr. Alexandre É. J. Yersin isolated and described the cause of plague—bacteria (later named *Yersinia pestis*) carried by the common flea. In most cases, plague entered the body when a flea injected the bacteria through the victim's skin. Early plague epidemics could have been controlled by the elimination of rats and the infected fleas they carried.

Dr. Ettenger knew that this illness from the past was no stranger to the United States. It had struck its first blow in 1900, when ships carrying plague-infected rats arrived in San Francisco from Hong Kong and Hawaii.

Soon after, the disease moved into the American countryside. There, infected fleas found new hosts: squirrels, chipmunks, rabbits, and prairie dogs. By 1949, New Mexico, with its high population of wild rodents, led all other states in number of reported cases of plague.

An ordinary case of plague wasn't unheard of in Gallup, but Jimmy Bistie's case was anything but ordinary. His strep throat had masked the early symptoms of the disease. More importantly, Jimmy had not developed "bubonic" plague, in which *Y. pestis* attacks the body's lymphatic system, producing large swellings, or "buboes," in the armpit or groin.

Jimmy had come down with *pneumonic* plague, possibly the world's most infectious and deadly form of pneumonia. The bacteria had invaded his lungs. During the last days of his life, with each breath and cough, Jimmy had sprayed with killer germs everyone crossing his path.

Dr. Ettenger recognized the extraordinary danger and wasted no time. She called the state department of health, who notified the Plague Branch, Vector-Borne Viral Diseases Division, of the Centers for Disease Control (CDC) in Fort Collins, Colorado.

Within hours, a pair of investigators arrived on the scene. The CDC men had worked on plague cases before. They knew its symptoms, its history, and where it was most likely to hide.

Their first task was to track down family, friends, neighbors, casual acquaintances, even the chanters Jimmy had visited. Aware that they were not a part of the Navajo community, the two investigators relied on the Indian Health Service for introductions and help with interviews.

The list was long, but no person or possibility was overlooked. Those at high risk, such as the nurse who had given Jimmy mouth-to-mouth resuscitation, were given antibiotics and treated as if they had the disease. Others were closely watched for symptoms.

As preventive measures lowered the risk of an epidemic, the investigators concentrated on the remaining part of the mystery. Where had the young Navajo picked up the disease? Again they relied on Jimmy's friends and family for answers.

Was Jimmy a hunter? The CDC had records of several cases in which hunters had come down with the plague after shooting and carrying away animals infested with plague-infected fleas.

But Jimmy did not hunt.

Did he have pets? There had been one case where a woman caught the plague after letting her flea-infested pet dogs sleep on her bed. In another instance, a veterinarian had developed plague after treating a sick cat.

Jimmy had no pets, but the family remembered that he had been fond of several neighborhood dogs and cats. In fact, they remembered that one cat had actually died in a car that Jimmy had been repairing.

This clue was promising, but led nowhere. The cat had died a month before Jimmy had become ill. If it had been the source of infection, he would have shown symptoms within a week or two.

Eliminating all other possibilities, the investigators were left with the most probable cause of Jimmy's illness—the prairie dogs that populated the countryside outside of Cuba. It was likely that infected fleas had multiplied on the small animals, hitchhiked a ride on a dog or cat that passed their way, and then made the relatively easy jump to Jimmy.

To prove their theory, the investigators needed to find out if plague was present in the neighborhood. Carefully, they set out small animal traps around Jimmy's trailer home.

The next day, the traps were empty.

This was intriguing. Ordinarily the countryside teemed with small animals. Even with plague in the neighborhood, prairie dogs and ground squirrels should have been present. In most cases, these animals could carry plague-infected fleas and still remain healthy.

Faced with their empty traps, the investigators knew they were tracking plague bacteria so lethal that nearly all of the animals in the district had died. The situation called for extra caution. Both men watched closely for flea bites and kept medication on hand in case they started to show symptoms.

Then they turned to the deserted burrows around Cuba. With a piece of white cloth attached to a hoselike instrument, they were able to reach deep inside the burrows. After fleas leaped onto the cloth, the men captured them and examined them for plague bacteria. To their satisfaction, a high proportion carried *Y. pestis*.

State authorities immediately began a flea-eradication program in the area. A month later, the numbers of plague-bearing fleas had dropped dramatically. By then, the crisis had passed. Seventy-four people had been at risk, but due to prompt preventative treatment, no one became ill.

• • • • •

Jimmy Bistie's death emphasized the hidden danger that innocent-looking wildlife could carry. A decade later, medical detectives remembered that danger as they set out to solve another baffling desert mystery. Again, dozens of lives were at stake.

On the evening of May 28, 1993, Kimberly Bartlett, a thirteen-year-old Navajo girl, arrived at a graduation party at Red Rock State Park, just outside Gallup, New Mexico. There was dancing and plenty of food. Kimberly's friends were all there. The celebration was living up to its promise of being a red-letter event.

But the party did not proceed as Kimberly, or anyone else, expected. As the shadows lengthened and Kimberly and her friends danced to the latest rock music, the young girl unexpectedly collapsed.

Bystanders, including Kimberly's mother, rushed to her aid. The situation appeared desperate. Kimberly was seriously ill. Her skin burned with fever. She struggled to breathe.

Park manager Sammy Trujillo reported his feeling of helplessness. "Her mother was screaming, 'Somebody save my child!' and there was nothing I could do."

Kimberly was rushed to the University of New Mexico Hospital in Albuquerque, about 125 miles (201 kilometers) away. There, doctors fought all night to save her life. The next day they lost their battle. Kimberly died.

What invisible agent had so suddenly and unexpectedly claimed the life of an ordinary, healthy person? Health officials had been searching for an answer to that question for more than a month, ever since the first cases of a flulike illness had cropped up in the region of the Navajo Reservation.

By the end of May, when Kimberly had become sick, the mysterious malady, known as "unexplained adult respiratory-distress syndrome," had grown to a regional epidemic. At least nineteen people had fallen ill. The death count stood at ten and was still rising. A majority of the victims were Navajo, most under age thirty. All had been in excellent health until the first symptoms appeared: high fever, muscle aches, cough, and (in some cases) eye infections. Then, within a few hours, their lungs filled with suffocating fluid. Too often, even prompt medical attention made no difference. The fact that the illness did not seem to be passed from person to person was the only bright spot in an otherwise gloomy picture.

As the news spread, many residents of the region panicked. Clinic and hospital waiting rooms overflowed with those who feared they might have the sickness. "My wife took the kids away . . . and says she's not going to come home until they find out what this thing is," the owner of a local business stated.

Outsiders worried that the illness might spread. In one instance, a Los Angeles private school cancelled a visit of Navajo schoolchildren for fear they might carry the infection.

Health officials, including the Indian Health Service, the New Mexico Department of Health, and the CDC, joined forces to solve the mystery. Investigators fanned out across the region, circulating questionnaires and asking questions.

At times, Navajo culture complicated their search. Families refused to allow autopsies and hesitated to speak of the dead for fear they might slow the spirit's trip to the afterlife. Elders claimed that tragedy had struck because many Navajo had forsaken the traditions of their ancestors. Medicine men recommended prayer and white corn pollen to cleanse the spirit, and herbal tea to clear the lungs.

The investigators remained scientific in their approach. Remembering that rodents were plague carriers, they trapped and examined many of the small animals. They combed pets and livestock for fleas and ticks that might be infected. They gathered samples of water, soil, plants, food, and drink to be tested for bacteria, viruses, fungi, and poisons. In the laboratory, researchers studied samples of blood and tissue from the victims.

One by one, diseases such as flu, plague, and Legionnaires' disease were ruled out, as were almost fifty other common and uncommon pathogens. Poisons were also eliminated.

Finally, the investigators' efforts were rewarded. In several of the victims, researchers discovered antibodies against hantaviruses, a group of viruses responsible for illness in the Far East. Experts had known that the viruses were present in America. However, they had never before been linked to serious human illness in the United States.

Circumstantial evidence also supported the hantavirus theory. Rodents were known to be carriers, able to harbor the virus without becoming sick. In 1993, because of unusually heavy spring rains, food supplies had been abundant in Arizona and New Mexico, and the rodent population had exploded. Victims usually contracted hantaviruses by inhaling airborne particles of infected rodent droppings, urine, or saliva. It would not have been unusual for the Navajo, many of whom lived close to the land, to come into contact with animal waste.

A few experts were not convinced. They pointed out that most viral infections with a sudden, severe onset, such as influenza, measles, and chicken pox, were extremely contagious. This infection was not. In addition, they argued, the symptoms shown here were not typical of other hantaviruses that attacked the kidneys, not the lungs.

Dr. James M. Hughes, director of the National Center for Infectious Diseases at the CDC, gave one possible explanation of the discrepancy. "We think it's a new strain of hantavirus. We're still keeping an open mind that other agents may be responsible, but right now hantavirus is by far our most promising lead."

State health officials hurried to issue news bulletins, warning residents of the danger posed by rodents and their droppings. Rodent control programs went into effect in areas with heavy infestations. Doctors were advised to use ribaviran, a drug effective against hantaviruses if given early enough, for new patients showing signs of respiratory distress.

The mystery was all but solved. Medical detectives could not undo the deaths, but they hoped that similar tragedy could be avoided in the future.

• • • • •

The threat of deadly disease in the Southwest cannot be taken lightly. In 1992 alone, at least ten cases of plague were reported. Plague-infected rodents, such as chipmunks and mice, are probably more numerous in North America today than were their ancestors in Eu-

As appealing as this little prairie dog is, he could easily be a carrier of the Black Death.

rope during the time of the Black Death. And, as the hantavirus epidemic proved, rodents may carry other equally dangerous organisms.

Modern scientists have not yet defeated these grim killers. But thanks to the dedication of doctors and health officials across the country, they can be tamed.

Chapter 7

Secrets in Steubenville

When Doctor David Taylor and his assistant, fourth-year medical student Emmett Schmidt, arrived in Steubenville, Ohio, at the end of January 1981, they faced an epidemic of food poisoning that had been in full swing for a month. Thirteen people were sick. More cases were reported every day.

The last thing Steubenville needed was an epidemic. A once-thriving steel town, it now sat, gray and alone, in a valley on the eastern edge of the state. Environmental regulation and reduced demand for steel had closed the mills. Unemployment ran high. As Taylor and Schmidt drove down the cheerless main street, their spirits sank.

But neither man was the kind to let a winter day get him down. As investigators for the Centers for Disease Control (CDC), they faced difficult conditions and mystifying cases almost every day. After checking into a motel, they headed straight for the local health department and began their search for the source of the infection.

First, they scanned reports put together by local health officials, who had already determined that the cases were caused by *Salmonella muenchen*, a fairly common strain of bacteria. No one had to explain *Salmonella* to the CDC men. They knew that it caused salmonellosis, the most common type of food poisoning in the world. Symptoms could include mild to severe nausea, vomiting, stomach cramps, diarrhea, and fever.

The reports indicated that the victims lived in three general locations: a neighborhood by the river, a housing tract called Winterville located on a hill above Steubenville, and a suburb of the town called Mingo Junction. Victims ranged in age from a one-month-old baby to a seventy-three-year-old grandmother.

The outbreak had been quite severe; 80 percent of the sick children and 65 percent of the infected adults had been hospitalized. No one had died yet, but the threat reared its ugly head with each new case that was reported.

Armed with these facts, Taylor and Schmidt got to work. From experience, they knew that most *Salmonella* epidemics have a common source—infected food from a restaurant, a picnic, a church potluck supper. The doctors began by talking to victims, looking for a thread that tied the whole problem together.

The first family contacted was the Lemings, a poor couple in the neighborhood by the river. The Leming baby was still recovering from the infection.

Mrs. Leming was young and nervous about talking to government officials. Having had a case of food poi-

The caps and gloves restaurant workers wear when
handling food might protect the patrons from the cooks,
but the bacteria that cause Salmonella *can live anywhere—*
on wood, plastic, or metal.

soning in her home troubled her. She had always tried
hard to keep a clean house. She was careful when she
cooked; careful to refrigerate all leftovers.

The doctors were soothing. They explained that
Salmonella often came straight from the grocery store
in processed or packaged foods. Meat from a deli-
catessen was often the culprit. Restaurant food was
suspect. They even knew of a case involving boxes of
chocolate candy.

Mrs. Leming informed them that she and her husband didn't eat in restaurants. They had no money for deli meat or candy. The best they had managed was a ham dinner for Christmas a few weeks back.

The doctors made a few notes and continued down the street to the Rundell home.

Pete Rundell, an out-of-work mill employee, was recovering from his bout of poisoning and seemed glad to have company. Yes, he and his wife were friends of the Lemings. They often got together to play cards. After all, when a man was out of work, he got kind of depressed, and there wasn't much money for having fun.

Before leaving, the doctors learned that the Rundell family had also eaten ham at Christmas.

The remaining interviews continued along the same lines. Two cases in the Winterville subdivision were high school students from well-to-do families. Neither seemed to have friends or activities in common. The Mingo Junction families were just as diverse.

Taylor and Schmidt had to admit that seldom had the clues, or lack of them, proved so exasperating. They consoled themselves with the thought that the investigation had just begun. Then they hit the streets again.

For days, their search led them from cafes to grocery stores, from bars to fast-food restaurants. They asked questions and took samples, then turned everything over to the lab for analysis.

Again, the results were disappointing. No *Salmonella;* everything was clean. Yet daily reports from doctors and hospitals indicated more cases regularly. The source of the epidemic was out there, as dangerous as ever.

Determinedly, the two men reviewed their notes,

looking for something all the victims had in common. The Christmas hams were the only slim possibility. Several families had listed ham on their holiday menus.

A second tour of the town's meat markets yielded no trace of *Salmonella*.

Then, late one night in his motel room, Taylor noticed something in his notes. A high number of teens and young adults were involved in the epidemic.

He and Schmidt checked the figures. In *Salmonella* epidemics nationwide, young adults made up about 12 percent of the total victims. In the Steubenville cases, they made up 28 percent. With a quick tally, the doctors found that a teen or young adult was present (but not always infected) in every *Salmonella* household.

Age certainly seemed to be a clue. Would it lead to an answer?

The doctors hoped it would. They had put in days of hard work, but the situation had become a tangle of tension and frustration. Health officials clamored for a quick solution. Restaurants and grocery stores, not yet cleared of suspicion, complained that they were losing business.

The doctors themselves were tired. Tired of motel beds and restaurant food. Tired of being separated from their families. At the end of one especially long day, Emmett Schmidt telephoned his wife and poured out his discouragement. What did she think? What could a bunch of young adults and teenagers have in common?

She gave a little laugh. What about drugs?

Schmidt blinked. It was a great suggestion. He mentioned the possibility to Taylor. The more they thought about it, the better it sounded. They had checked everything else. Drugs, even prescription drugs, could be contaminated as easily as food or drink.

Excited by the possibilities, the two men set out on the interview circuit again. This time they began with the Rundells.

After chatting for a few minutes, Taylor came to the point. He wondered if anyone in the family took drugs of any kind.

Mrs. Rundell frowned. Medications? No, the family was pretty healthy, except for the food poisoning.

Taylor paused. What about illegal drugs?

Certainly not. Mrs. Rundell's face reddened.

Her husband was less nervous. He grinned. Maybe they used a little marijuana but nothing else. Being out of work was very stressful. Smoking pot with a few friends—the Lemings bought their marijuana from the same dealer—helped them relax.

The two doctors exchanged glances. Would there be a possibility of getting a sample of the drug for testing?

A little reluctantly, Rundell went into the bedroom and came back with some marijuana in an envelope. The doctors took it carefully. For the first time in weeks, they believed they were holding solid evidence in their hands.

Down the street, Mrs. Leming was even more flustered by their visit this time. The men soon assured her that they were not connected with the police and that helping them in their investigation would not land her in any kind of trouble.

They left with a plastic bag of marijuana safely stashed in Taylor's jacket pocket.

Leaving the marijuana at the lab for analysis, Taylor and Schmidt set off for Winterville and Mingo

Drugs such as marijuana are seldom "pure." Fillers used in cutting the product can be contaminated, and poisoning can be the result.

Junction. In both places, victims confessed that they had smoked marijuana or knew friends or family who did. It was surprisingly easy to get hold of samples to send to the lab.

Taylor broke the news to the medical community and the press shortly thereafter. The case appeared to be a first—a *Salmonella* epidemic caused by contaminated marijuana.

The CDC investigators were flooded with questions. How had the marijuana been contaminated? Where had it come from? Why had babies and old people gotten sick when they obviously had not used the drug?

Taylor could only guess at the first two answers. The severity of the infection made him suspect that the drug had been cut, or diluted, with contaminated animal manure. Manure was often used by drug dealers to increase the weight of the product, thus increasing the profits.

Taylor also believed that the drug had come from Colombia or Jamaica, major marijuana suppliers to the United States. During their stay at Steubenville, he and Schmidt had received word of other mystery *Salmonella* epidemics across the country. Thanks to the Steubenville findings, these epidemics proved to be caused by contaminated marijuana as well. Only a major dealer could have supplied so many states with the same polluted product.

Taylor's last answer was followed by a warning. The high level of infection in this case caused even nonusers (especially small children) to become sick after only touching or kissing someone who handled the drug. Taylor reminded the public that illegal drugs are not subject to the government health and safety regulations that apply to all prescription and over-the-counter drugs.

In any illegal drug transaction, the danger of contamination from disease, poison, or other drugs was high. Let the buyer beware!

Taylor and Schmidt's work in Steubenville was finished. Before returning to Atlanta, they took one last look at the town that had appeared so innocent, so isolated from the rest of the world.

The doctors shook their heads as they drove away. For them, the town had revealed some of its secrets. They would never forget the mystery of Steubenville.

Chapter 8

Ghosts from the Past

Ray Balmer's thirty-fifth birthday was not a happy one. There was no party, no dinner at his favorite restaurant, not even a simple get-together with friends. Ray found it hard to eat a small dish of ice cream and cake while wearing the blue mask that covered his nose and mouth. Without it, his family ran the risk of catching the lethal bacteria he carried.

Ray had been sick for several months, but his problem began many years before. In the 1950s, his father had returned from the Korean War with tuberculosis (TB), an infection of the lungs. No one in the family had been overly concerned. The disease was no longer the dreaded killer it had been earlier in the century. The chance of being cured was high.

Unfortunately, Ray's father had fought a losing battle against TB. Newly developed antibiotics failed to work. He died several years later, but not before unknowingly passing the bacteria on to Ray.

With no cough, fatigue, or other symptoms, Ray carried the latent infection until 1991, when he was thirty-four years old. Then the tuberculosis became active with a vengeance.

Doctors quarantined Ray in his Tennessee home while they tried drug after drug to cure him. He endured painful shots three times a week. He had surgery to drain fluid from one lung.

In spite of all that, the persistent bacteria continued to eat away at his body. He lost weight, was short of breath, and felt tired all the time. His friends deserted him for fear of catching the deadly infection.

At last, in a desperate effort to save Ray's life, his doctors sent him to the National Jewish Center for Immunology and Respiratory Medicine in Denver, Colorado, one of the most progressive tuberculosis hospitals in the nation. Ray allowed himself to hope for a cure. Dr. Michael Iseman, an expert in the disease, had taken on his case. With luck, and a lot of determination, Ray had a chance to survive.

• • • • •

The battle against tuberculosis had already been fought before in the United States. At the turn of the century, Americans called it "consumption" or the "White Plague," and knew that catching it meant almost certain death. There was no cure. Worse yet, the infection could be passed quite easily through the air when bacteria were coughed up from the lungs of an infected person and inhaled by a healthy one.

Authorities responded to public fear by isolating TB patients from the rest of the population. The poor were often sent west to tent cities in Arizona or hauled off by police to overcrowded hospitals like the Riverside Sanitarium on North Brother Island in New York.

*In 1918 these children suffering from tuberculosis were sent
away from their families to the Sunny Acres Sanatorium
in Cleveland, Ohio.*

Well-to-do patients went to the mountains—sometimes
as far away as Switzerland—for the fresh air and rest
that was believed to help them recover.

The first antibiotic—streptomycin—came on the
scene in 1943. Now doctors had something that could
actually wipe out *Mycobacterium tuberculosis*, the
bacteria that German researcher Robert Koch had
identified in 1882. The death rate began to drop.

By 1960, thanks to improved living conditions,
early diagnosis, and antitubercular drugs, TB had be-

come an almost forgotten disease. In 1988 the Centers for Disease Control (CDC) issued "A Strategic Plan for the Elimination of Tuberculosis in the United States." They hoped TB would be a thing of the past by the year 2010.

That hope had faded by the early 1990s. In 1985 there had been only 22,000 new cases of TB reported in the United States. In 1991 there were nearly 27,000 new cases, and the number was growing annually. Most frightening was the increasing number of infections that did not respond to treatment, such as the one that plagued Ray Balmer.

All signs pointed to an epidemic in the making. Anxious health care workers asked themselves what had gone wrong. Why was TB making a comeback? More importantly, what could they do to stop it?

Researchers and scientists at the CDC, helped by specialists like Dr. Iseman and a host of doctors and nurses who faced the disease every day, began to look for answers that would solve this troubling mystery.

The first piece of the puzzle was disturbing, but not unexpected. Tuberculosis was on the rise among the growing number of poor people in America. This group, which included minorities, the mentally ill, and the old, had always been at high risk to catch the disease. They often lived in unhealthy, overcrowded conditions and failed to get proper medical care.

As this population increased, so did the need for public health programs that could combat diseases like tuberculosis. In spite of that, fewer were available.

Investigators noted that funds set aside to fight tuberculosis had been cut. New York City hospitals that once supported a total of one thousand beds for TB patients now could maintain fewer than seventy-five.

Where once there were twenty-two full-time TB clinics, only nine remained, most of them run down and overcrowded.

Institutions that did treat tuberculosis patients often failed to provide safeguards that would keep the disease from spreading. Few wards were equipped with specially ventilated rooms or ultraviolet lights that killed bacteria in the air. In one New York hospital, CDC investigators were shocked to find TB patients wandering the halls or sitting in lounges, chatting with uninfected friends. Even the simple precaution of wearing a face mask had been neglected.

"We've not been too wise over the years," admitted Dr. Dixie Snider, director of the Division of Tuberculosis Control at the CDC.

The second piece of the puzzle disturbed the investigators even more than the first. Overwhelming evidence revealed that people with Acquired Immune Deficiency Syndrome (AIDS), whose immune systems were weakened, were becoming infected with TB at a terrifying rate. New York City health officials estimated that people with the AIDS virus made up at least 25 percent of the city's new TB cases every year.

Further bad news added to the bleak picture. Not only were AIDS patients at higher risk to catch TB, they were more difficult to cure, more likely to develop symptoms (especially a cough), and, therefore, more likely to pass TB to others. As might be expected, people with AIDS had a much greater chance of dying from TB than did patients without AIDS. The disease, already a national tragedy, was a disastrous complication in the tuberculosis crisis as well.

Investigators found that the third piece of the puzzle was related to the nature of the bacteria itself.

Doctors had long ago discovered that *Mycobacterium tuberculosis* seemed able to mutate quite rapidly, developing resistance to antibiotics almost overnight.

But the problem of drug-resistance had become worse as thousands of patients—many of them homeless, mentally ill, or addicted to drugs—stopped taking medication before the disease was totally eliminated from their system. Before long, they were contagious again, this time with an infection that was harder to cure.

Louisa, a twenty-five-year-old Manhattan cocaine addict, had been in and out of city health clinics and hospitals with resistant tuberculosis for two years. Workers had begged, telephoned, even bribed her with Oreos, her favorite cookies, to encourage her to finish treatment. But Louisa always stopped taking the medication that she claimed made her feel worse instead of better.

With each unfinished treatment, the organisms that survived in her lungs—those most resistant to antibiotics—multiplied, making her infection more difficult to control the next time it occurred. In addition, each person that Louisa infected carried those same resistant organisms.

Poverty, AIDS, and drug abuse were putting a strain on inadequate health programs and a shrinking inventory of drugs used to fight tuberculosis. Investigators had found answers to the first part of the puzzle. A further, and more important, question was—What next? And what could be done to control the growing epidemic?

The first, and most obvious, solution involved making better use of all available resources. The disease had to be recognized for the real danger it repre-

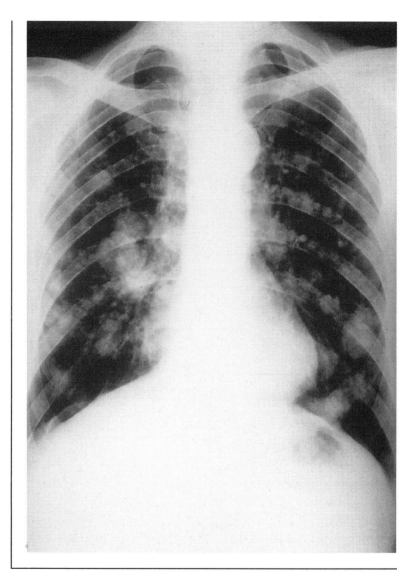

An X ray clearly shows shadows in the lungs indicating TB.
Suddenly doctors are seeing more and more X rays like this.

sented. People at risk needed to be screened and then, if necessary, treated until they were well again.

Experts urged that treatment guidelines be made a top priority for TB control, especially for doctors who were unaware of the most up-to-date methods of defeating the disease. Dr. Eran Bellin, head of medical services in a large New York prison system, observed, "They do it one way at Columbia [medical school]. Another at Cornell. I have my own . . . mix. We really need . . . better guidance."

Dr. Iseman, whose determination and creativity achieved a 90 percent cure rate with almost hopelessly resistant cases in Denver, agreed that pooling information and ideas was necessary. Year after year, he shared his expertise in training sessions for health professionals around the country, and received more than nine hundred phone calls annually for advice in treatment. "Think about it, it makes sense," he declared.

• • • • •

Everyone agreed that doctors and hospitals should work together to help solve the problem. But what was to be done with the thousands of people, like Louisa, who refused to take advantage of what was already available?

The thought of one TB patient infecting dozens of unsuspecting people had already frightened some officials into drastic action. In spite of protests that rights were being violated, they ordered uncooperative patients placed in hospitals and given treatment whether they wanted it or not.

Dr. Thomas Frieden, head of New York City's Bureau of TB Control, criticized this approach. ". . . When people are scared they grab for a simple answer. And locking sick people away is a simple answer. Simple, quick and wrong."

Dr. Iseman, too, was convinced that there were better ways to get patients to take their medicine. In Denver, where he practiced, tuberculosis had been brought under control thanks to the city's reward system, which gave free lunches, food coupons, and transportation to patients who kept their appointments at TB clinics. The overall cost proved small compared with the thousands of dollars necessary to treat one drug-resistant case.

Care, cooperation, and creativity would go far to curb the rising tuberculosis crisis in America, but investigators were quick to point out that existing programs were not enough.

Health workers could cope with the growing number of cases only if additional, improved clinics and hospital facilities were provided. Specially ventilated rooms were essential if infectious patients were to be isolated from others in the hospitals. Up-to-date lab equipment was indispensable for quick diagnoses and to keep track of patients' progress.

In addition to new equipment, research was vital to discover new weapons that doctors could use to fight the disease. Scientists needed to know more about the make-up of the bacteria itself. Better medicines to combat drug-resistant forms were a necessity. The Bacillus Calmette-Guérin (BCG) vaccine, named for its developers in 1921, did not protect against the disease, only lowered the risk of complications. Development and distribution of an effective vaccine was long overdue.

Finally, money was all-important in order for the fight to continue. One specially designed isolation room might cost as much as $450,000. Drugs and therapy to cure one person of drug-resistant TB usually exceeded $250,000. Yet officials were only beginning to set aside funds to fight the disease. New York City claimed it would raise at least $100 million to be spent on TB in 1993. The federal government planned to set aside only $74.3 million for the rest of the nation for that same period.

• • • • •

Tuberculosis, a ghost from the past, has arisen to haunt America again. Finding solutions to this difficult and controversial problem promises to be a formidable task. Still, the need for action is obvious and long overdue.

Experts would like to think that given time, talent, and cooperation, the disease can be successfully subdued, just as it was before. "It's a winnable battle," says Dr. Frieden. "We know what has to be done. We just don't know whether we as a society will be able to do it."

If we do, we will be wise to find a way to make certain that the ghost never walks again.

Doctor Tom McDevitt will never forget the winter of
1967, the winter that a mysterious illness battered his
family and almost took their lives.

The trouble began after Christmas, while Tom was
working hard at a veterans' hospital in Los Angeles. At
first, he felt a little under the weather. His head ached.
His stomach hurt now and then.

As days passed, Tom's wife, Bruna, complained of
the same symptoms. She was barely able to tend their
four small children and complete her daily chores. The
children felt just as bad. Usually they ate everything in
sight, but now they pushed their food away half eaten.
Little things made them cry. Only the baby remained
happy and hungry.

"I guess we all have a touch of the flu," Tom told
Bruna. "There's been a lot of it around this winter."

The weeks went on, but no one seemed to get
better. In spite of that, Bruna insisted on having a
birthday party for their oldest son, Sean, who would be

turning four. The celebration was simple, but the neighborhood children she invited seemed delighted to eat ice cream and cake and romp in the backyard.

Sean, the birthday boy, did not share their delight. He was cranky and hard to please. Before the party ended, he squabbled with another little boy, who pushed him down. Crying, Sean ran to show his mother the "goose-egg" lump swelling his forehead. Bruna ended the unfortunate party soon after that.

Later that evening, Tom went in to check on the children and found Sean vomiting. While he tenderly changed his son's pajamas, Tom noticed something that sent a chill up his spine. Sean could not move one of his legs. After a closer check, Tom realized that the entire left side of Sean's body was paralyzed.

The young doctor immediately remembered the fall at the party. In medical school, he had studied brain injuries and knew that paralysis could be the result of a broken blood vessel and possible serious bleeding in the brain. If that was the case, pressure would build up. Sean needed immediate attention or he could die.

Tom rushed his son to the hospital where a medical team checked the boy's pulse, temperature, and blood pressure, and drew a small amount of blood for tests that might throw light on the problem. The results of the tests did not explain the paralysis. Instead they revealed something totally unexpected. Sean had severe anemia (low numbers of oxygen-carrying cells in the blood, causing a feeling of weakness or tiredness). He also appeared to be malnourished.

If Tom had not been so concerned, he would have been embarrassed. Bruna was a good cook, always serving well-balanced meals. There was no reason Sean should be so weak.

Still, Tom's worry about the paralysis overshadowed everything else. He listened as Duke Hanna, a neurosurgeon at the hospital, explained that the best course would be immediate exploratory surgery. (Advanced technology such as CAT scans—X rays combined with computerized analysis of the brain—would have spared Sean this hazardous procedure today.) If the problem was internal bleeding, surgery would relieve the pressure on the little boy's brain.

Brain surgery on their four-year-old! The thought was terrifying to Tom and Bruna. But Dr. Hanna was well qualified, and Sean's life was at stake. Breathlessly they waited until, a few hours later, the neurosurgeon told them their son was out of danger. The operation had disclosed no pressure and no bleeding. Sean had been given a blood transfusion to help correct his anemia. There was still an outside chance that his paralysis was due to a brain tumor, but they would wait and see if the symptoms continued.

Weeks later, Sean returned home. The traumatic experience seemed to have worked a miracle. Not only had his paralysis disappeared, he was more energetic and his appetite had improved. Bruna and Tom, still not in the best of health, kept a close watch over their son, but it was hard to remember the pale, irritable child of a few months before.

All went well for a short time. But soon Bruna noticed that Sean's condition had changed for the worse. His rosy cheeks were fading, along with his energy. She complained to Tom that the boy was only picking at his food again.

Tom hardly listened. His attention had focused on Margie, normally a lively and bossy three-year-old. Now she seemed weakest of the children, often sitting and crying over nothing.

Remembering a family history of diabetes, Tom scheduled lab tests for his little daughter. She had been pronounced healthy at her last physical, but a child grew and changed so rapidly.

In a few days, the lab reports were back. They were as disturbing as Sean's had been a few weeks before. Margie didn't have diabetes. She, too, was seriously anemic.

Tom could scarcely believe the news. He ordered the tests rerun. On the spur of the moment, he asked the lab to draw some of his own blood and test it as well.

Later that day, the hospital's chief pathologist (a specialist in the cause and nature of disease) called Tom to his office.

"Dr. McDevitt, both you and your daughter are very anemic," he announced. "I strongly suspect that you are being poisoned."

Tom was speechless. His head whirled as the doctor went on. Tests showed extremely high doses of lead in both his and Margie's blood. As Tom knew, lead was a metal that could affect the nerves, the stomach, the kidneys, and the bones. Children were especially at risk—their brains could be damaged, their growth stunted.

The doctor reminded Tom that the human body stores lead over time. Even small amounts of the substance, taken regularly, would eventually lead to lethal levels.

"You have about reached your limit," the doctor concluded gravely.

Tom's confused mind stopped whirling. Suddenly, his family's symptoms all made sense. Sean's anemia, the tiredness, the irritability, the stomach pains, all were classic symptoms of lead poisoning. Tom was willing to bet any amount of money that the health of the whole family was in the same dangerous condition.

Anxiously, he brought Bruna and the children in for a complete series of tests. Then he set to work to find a solution to the problem that threatened his family. Where was the poison coming from?

He first turned to the plumbing in his home. During his medical studies, he had learned that lead water pipes were a leading cause of lead poisoning in many families. As a double check, he also had his water tested. The results were negative. The pipes and water were lead-free.

Next he checked the house for lead paint. Studies had shown that babies could develop high levels of lead from chewing on windowsills or crib rails covered with leaded paint.

This also proved to be a dead end, but Tom had expected that. Both he and Bruna were being poisoned, too, and neither of them had gnawed on anything painted since they were babies more than twenty years ago.

While Tom ruled out the obvious possibilities, lab tests proved that Sean's paralysis had been due to the poisoning, not an accident or a tumor. They also confirmed the diagnosis of lead poisoning in the entire family—with one exception. The baby showed no signs of poisoning at all.

Tom and Bruna's surprise and relief for their youngest was swallowed up in worry. She might be well today, but what about tomorrow? Identifying the family's problem hadn't helped solve it. With each passing day, the danger increased. Unless they found the source of the poison soon . . .

"Get out of your house," the pathologist advised. "It may be the only way to save your lives."

Locally made clayware for sale on the street in Mexico. The brilliant colored glazes add beauty—and often an insidious health risk—to the pottery.

Sick and depressed, the McDevitts began house hunting. In the back of their minds, the worry remained. Where was the poison coming from? What if they unknowingly packed it up and took it with them when they moved?

The thought tormented Tom. He eyed every item he touched with suspicion.

One morning, while watching Bruna pour juice for the children, his eyes focused on the brown ceramic pitcher in her hand.

The pitcher, made in Mexico, had been a Christmas gift from a friend. Bruna loved its earthy, handmade appearance and used it regularly to hold the family's juice.

A memory stirred in the back of Tom's mind. Years ago in high school, he had learned something about lead being an ingredient in ceramic glazes.

The puzzle clicked. Everyone but the baby, who was too young, drank juice from the pitcher. Everyone but the baby was being poisoned.

Tom set off for the hospital, pitcher in hand. It was sent for analysis to the Santa Monica Public Health Department. The next day a health officer handed Tom a small bag full of white powder.

"Pure lead chromate," he told Tom. "Enough to kill two people. It came out of your pitcher in just one washing with acid."

Tom, Bruna, and the children had to undergo several long and uncomfortable blood-cleansing treatments before all the lead was removed from their bodies. After several weeks they found themselves almost as good as new. In time, they recovered their appetites, their health, and their zest for life.

• • • • •

The end of the McDevitt's ordeal is not the end of the lead poisoning story. The passing of time has lessened, but not eliminated, the hazards.

Following his brush with death, Tom McDevitt took action to protect others from the danger of improperly glazed pottery. As a result of his efforts, the Food and Drug Administration set limits on the amount of lead acceptable in ceramic products. Those regulations, however, do not apply to ceramic ware made in Mexico, China, Portugal, Italy, or Spain. These imports remain a very real source of danger to the public.

Water pipes in some older homes, and walls and furniture covered with lead-based paint, also continue to present a health threat to many Americans.

Doctors are now aware that even low levels of lead in the body can be dangerous. Experts urge that all one-year-old children be tested for lead poisoning. At the same time, they continue to lower the level at which patients should go in for treatment of the condition.

Chance forced Tom McDevitt to take on the role of medical detective. Determination helped him expose a hidden killer and save the lives of his family. His story has benefited thousands who might otherwise have suffered or died from a case of "pretty poison."

Chapter 10

*Victims
of the Night*

Nao Shua Thao escaped death the first time when he
fled from the ruthless Communist takeover of Laos, his
Southeast Asian homeland, in 1976. He escaped again
when he left the harsh and unhealthy conditions of a
refugee camp in neighboring Thailand and made his
way to the United States, settling with his wife and
children in a tiny apartment in Chicago.

The third time, in the early morning hours of September 16, 1982, Nao Shua Thao was not so lucky.

It had been mid-July when Nao Shua and his family entered the country. Medical officials, performing a
health check on all immigrants, discovered that Nao
Shua's wife, Yang Cher, suffered from a goiter (an enlargement of the thyroid gland, visible as a swelling on
the front of her neck). Surgery was recommended. Two
months later, on the afternoon of September 14, 1982,
Nao Shua escorted his wife to a local hospital to correct
the problem.

Both husband and wife were nervous. In Laos, they had been part of the Hmong tribe, simple farmers who put their faith in folk remedies and spirits. Neither could speak English, and the language barrier made it impossible to communicate their fears. Nevertheless, both wanted to be good citizens in their new country. They were careful to cause no trouble.

With Yang Cher in the hospital, Nao Shua found it hard to relax. However, on the evening of September 15, the night before the surgery, he went to bed early and dropped into an exhausted sleep. Sometime after midnight, one of his sons, who shared the same room, was awakened by muffled sounds coming from the bed. Thinking that his father was dreaming, the boy turned over and went back to sleep.

The next morning, Chua Lee, the oldest son, tried to awaken his father. His attempts failed. Nao Shua was dead.

Nao Shua Thao was not the first to die in such an unexpected and mysterious way. He was only one of dozens of Southeast Asian refugees who had fallen prey to an epidemic of death developing in the United States.

The episodes seemed to have begun in 1977, but the growing numbers went unreported until 1981. Then, by chance, a medical examiner in Portland, Oregon, noticed that two refugees had died within days of each other in his city. Their stories had been the same as Nao Shua's—apparently healthy men went to bed at night and, with scarcely a sound, died in their sleep.

As word of the deaths spread, a nationwide investigation began. In February 1981 the Centers for Disease Control (CDC) became involved. Dr. Roy Baron took charge of the case.

Wasting no time, Dr. Baron and his team of disease detectives started the hunt by reviewing past cases and asking themselves what qualities the dead refugees had in common.

The answers weren't hard to find. Significant facts repeated themselves over and over again. The victims in every case were Southeast Asian men between the ages of nineteen and fifty-four. At least half had belonged to the Hmong tribe.

All had been healthy. The majority had been sleeping peacefully when, with a low moan or a gurgle, they died. Attempts to revive them almost always failed. In each case, autopsies (examination of the body to determine cause of death) revealed no signs of heart disease. No elusive and deadly virus had been identified. No obvious diseases or weaknesses showed up.

One medical examiner said it best. "In each case, we asked ourselves what they had died from and the answer was 'Nothing.'"

With plenty of tantalizing evidence, but no solutions, the detectives turned to another part of the mystery of sudden, unexplained nocturnal death (SUND). Why had the deaths occurred where and when they did?

Early findings had indicated that the refugees died within weeks of arriving in the United States. If this were so, Dr. Baron guessed that the team should be looking for some factor in their new American lifestyle.

But continuing research, including interviews with victims' families, seemed to cast doubt on that theory. Many victims, like Nao Shua, were recent arrivals. Others, like thirty-seven-year-old Khammon Ankhavong, had lived in their new communities for more than a year.

Laotian immigrants participate in a traditional wedding ceremony. The sudden, unexplained, nocturnal death suffered by male Laotian refugees appeared to have nothing to do with their adjustment to life in this country.

A CDC investigator traveled to Seattle, Washington, to talk to Khammon Ankhavong's widow, Khao. She refuted suggestions that her husband had been longing to return to his homeland. In fact, he had learned to love his new country. His goal had been to learn the English language and get a better job.

The investigator nodded sympathetically. Had her husband ever been sick? Had she noticed anything unusual about him that night? Had she any ideas about the cause of his death?

Khao shook her head. Khammon had always enjoyed good health. He had perhaps fallen asleep a little earlier than usual that night, but there had been no sign of his impending death. That was the way it went, she said, with "sleeping death." In Laos, seven of Khammon's male relatives had died under just such conditions.

The news was a jolt to the investigation. The team now knew that whatever had killed Nao Shua, Khammon Ankhavong, and the others had existed in their old world as well.

Months passed. Work on the case continued, and the deaths mounted. By July 1985, more than eighty cases were recorded in the United States. October 1987 brought the total to more than one hundred. New reports of similar deaths in other parts of the world, notably refugee camps in Thailand, confirmed Khao's information and swelled the numbers.

Still, the mystery remained unsolved. "We are in the process of describing something that has not been identified before in Western culture," Dr. Baron pointed out, as theory after theory was proposed and discarded.

Those theories were as varied as they were numerous.

Some health authorities suggested that the victims suffered from sleep apnea, a temporary halt in breathing (often related to snoring) that produces irregular heartbeats. Nao Shua's son had testified that his father had made unusual sounds just before he died. Yet the CDC investigators could find no evidence that the victims had suffered from the disorder prior to their deaths. Numerous cases of unexpected, deadly apnea seemed an unlikely solution.

Other researchers pointed out that many victims had complained of frightening dreams before they died. Had a terrifying nightmare scared the refugees to death?

Thirty-five-year-old Ge Xiong, one of the few men to be resuscitated from his near-death experience, reported having one such dream some time before his attack. But investigators discovered that on that night, Ge Xiong remembered having no such dream. And if he had? Dr. Baron noted that everyone has nightmares. There is no evidence that anyone ever died from them.

The refugees themselves had their own theories. Some blamed "yellow rain," chemical warfare practiced during the Vietnam conflict. Dr. Baron disagreed. Chemical poisons affected women as well as men. Besides that, no trace of poisons or chemicals had been found in the victims' bodies.

Other refugees wanted to blame demons or other supernatural beings for the tragedies. Because they came from a different culture, some misunderstood Western technology and feared that "evil spirits" dwelling in television sets were responsible. A few claimed that the souls of the victims had been taken by "widow ghosts" searching for husbands.

Being scientists, Dr. Baron and his team did not consider supernatural theories, but they admitted that one unexplored factor—stress—could easily have played a part in the mystery.

Nao Shua's life, with its long periods of danger and uncertainty, had been a perfect example.

So had Khammon Ankhavong's. He had survived the war in his country, only to be labeled an enemy of the new Communist government and sent to a camp for three years of "retraining." After a daring escape, he had fled the country with his family, leaving everything behind.

In the United States, Khammon had faced new challenges. In Laos, he and his family had been Buddhists; in America, he tried to please his sponsor by attending a Protestant church. In Laos, he had been a well-educated civil servant; in the United States, he settled for work as a baker's assistant.

There was no doubt that Nao Shua Thao, Khammon Ankhavong, and thousands of others like them had lived under a heavy burden of stress. But Dr. Baron's team did not believe that stress alone was killing the refugees.

Sifting through the reports, they wondered for the thousandth time what the answer might be. What mysterious foe struck only during sleep? Why did it condemn men but spare women who had suffered equal hardships?

The team hoped for a breakthrough. But as fewer Asian refugees came to the United States, and as earlier refugees grew more comfortable in their new world, the number of cases dropped. Attention turned to refugee camps in Asia where the deaths continued at a higher rate. The search became a worldwide effort.

• • • • •

Unlike other mysteries in this book, the cause of the refugees' sudden death is at present unknown. The clues are perplexing. Many questions remain unanswered.

The case has been long and grueling, but investigators still hope for a breakthrough. Possibly, some determined scientist will uncover a new organism, a hidden weakness, or a combination of factors that sheds new light on the problem. The end of the search may be just around the corner. Perhaps it will make headlines in the newspaper tomorrow.

If not, the medical detectives will go on searching. They will not walk away from an unsolved mystery.

Notes

... later tallies would show that more than 150 people ...
> David W. Fraser, "Legionnaires' Disease." *The New England Journal of Medicine*, 1 December 1977, 1189–1197.

"It was an environment in which it was hard to do science or anything else."
> David W. Fraser, quoted in Allen B. Weisse, *Medical Odysseys* (New Brunswick, N.J.: Rutgers University Press, 1991), 199.

"I was getting a hundred calls a day ..."
> Dr. Renate Kimbrough, quoted in Charles Gregg, *A Virus of Love and Other Tales of Medical Mystery* (New York: Charles Scribner's Sons, 1983), 179.

A total of 182 people had become ill ...
> David W. Fraser et al, "Legionnaires' Disease," *The New England Journal of Medicine*, 1 December 1977, 1189–1197.

"I despaired that we'd solve it."
> David W. Fraser, quoted in Gerald Astor, *The Disease Detectives* (New York: New American Library, Inc. 1983), 27.

... bacteria is still a threat, striking an estimated 50,000 Americans every year.
> Allen B. Weisse, *Medical Odysseys* (New Brunswick, N.J.: Rutgers University Press, 1991), 210.

Chapter Two

(Polly Murray's story is also recounted in Diana Benzaia's book, *Protect Yourself From Lyme Disease*.)

"I began having periodic flu-like illnesses . . . ," "I was convinced that everyone in the family had the same thing . . . ," "I worried about what we all might be eating . . . ," "It seemed . . . strange for so many children . . ."
> Polly Murray, quoted in Diana Benzaia, *Protect Yourself From Lyme Disease* (New York: Dell Publishing, 1989), 10–13.

"We checked them all. Food, water, drugs, immunizations, other diseases, pets—you name it."
> Allen Steere, quoted in Boyce Rensberger, "A New Type of Arthritis Found in Lyme," *The New York Times*, 18 July, 1976.

Chapter Three

(Details of the first incidents of bat rabies in the United States are drawn from Berton Roueché's *The Medical Detectives*.)

"encephalomyelitis with demonstrable Negri bodies . . ."
> Edward S. Sulkin and Marion J. Greve, "Human Rabies Caused by Bat Bite," *Texas State Journal of Medicine* (August 1954), 620–621.

. . . poppy tears, Illyrian iris, Gallic nard . . .

Aulus Cornelius Celsus, *De Medicina*, trans. W. G. Spencer (Cambridge, Mass.: Harvard University Press, 1953). Also quoted in Berton Roueché, *The Medical Detectives* (New York: Times Books, 1981).

"Carlsbad Cave Bats Infected With Rabies," *Santa Fe New Mexican*, 1 February 1956.

Of seven cases of human rabies that occurred in the United States between 1980 and 1991, five were caused by bats.

"Human Rabies—Texas, Arkansas, Georgia, 1991," *Journal of the American Medical Association*, 4 December 1991, 2956.

New York State listed 225 cases of reported animal rabies in 1991, as compared with 54 in 1989. Animals that posed the greatest danger included red foxes, skunks, and raccoons.

"Guarding Against Bats With Rabies," *The New York Times*, 26 May 1991.

The Tilson case has replaced Donald Bright's as the first occurrence of bat rabies in the United States.

Edward S. Sulkin and Marion J. Greve, "Human Rabies Caused by Bat Bite," *Texas State Journal of Medicine*, August 1954, 620–621.

Chapter Four

By May 1981, the number stood at five . . .

Mirko Grmek, *History of AIDS* (Princeton, N.J.: Princeton University Press, 1990), 4.

By March 1981, at least eight cases had been identified . . .

Mirko Grmek, *History of AIDS* (Princeton, N.J.: Princeton University Press, 1990), 6.

A CDC report, dated July 3, 1981, set out the early findings . . .

Frederick Siegal and Marta Siegal, *AIDS: The Medical Mystery* (New York: Grove Press, 1984), 215.

"Physicians should be alert for Kaposi's sarcoma, *Pneumocystis carinii* pneumonia, and other . . . infections associated with immunosuppression in homosexual men."
Frederick Siegal and Marta Siegal, *AIDS: The Medical Mystery* (New York: Grove Press, 1984), 217.

The number of cases, and deaths, kept climbing . . .
Frederick Siegal and Marta Siegal, *AIDS: The Medical Mystery* (New York: Grove Press, 1984), 217.

. . . with ten cases being reported each week . . .
Mirko Grmek, *History of AIDS* (Princeton, N.J.: Princeton University Press, 1990), 40.

Chapter Five

(The story of the poisoned jeans is drawn from Berton Roueché's *The Medical Detectives.)*

"County Warns Salvage Jeans Contain Poison."
The Fresno Bee, 25 October, 1961.

Chapter Six

(Jimmy Bistie's story is drawn from Gerald Astor's *The Disease Detectives.*)

It had struck its first blow in 1900, when ships carrying plague-infected rats . . .
Charles Gregg, *Plague, An Ancient Disease in the Twentieth Century* (Albuquerque, N.M.: University of New Mexico Press, 1985): 39.

By 1949, New Mexico . . . led all other states in number of reported cases of plague.
Charles Gregg, *Plague, An Ancient Disease in the Twentieth Century* (Albuquerque, N.M.: University of New Mexico Press, 1985): 210.

Seventy-four people had been at risk . . .
Gerald Astor, *The Disease Detectives* (New York: New American Library, Inc., 1983): 156.

"Her mother was screaming, 'Somebody save my child!' and there was nothing I could do."

Sammy Trujillo, quoted in Anastasia Toufexis, "Evil Over the Land, *Time*, 14 June 1993.

At least nineteen people had become sick. The death count stood at ten and was still rising.

Michael Haederle, "Navajo Area Is Sifted for Clues to Fatal Disease," *The Los Angeles Times*, 31 May 1993.

"My wife took the kids away . . .

Bruce Burch, quoted in Natalie Angier, "In Navajo Land of Mysteries, One Carried a Deadly Illness," *The New York Times*, 5 June 1993.

Medicine men recommended prayer and white corn . . .

Dan McGraw, "A Desert Killer, A Culture Clash," *U.S. News & World Report*, 14 June 1993.

"We think it's a new strain of hantavirus. We're still keeping an open mind that other agents may be responsible, but right now hantavirus is by far our most promising lead."

Dr. James M. Hughes, quoted in Natalie Angier, "Tracks of Mystery Disease Lead to New Form of Virus," *The New York Times*, 11 June 1993.

Chapter Seven

(Details of the Steubenville mystery can be found in Berton Roueché's *The Medical Detectives, Volume Two*.)

. . . an epidemic of food poisoning that had been in full swing for a month. Thirteen people were sick. More cases were reported every day.
The outbreak had been quite severe . . .

Roueché, Berton. *The Medical Detectives, Volume Two* (New York: E. P. Dutton, Inc., 1984), 331–333.

Schmidt telephoned his wife. . . . What did she think? . . . She gave a little laugh. What about drugs?

Gerald Astor, *The Disease Detectives* (New York: New American Library, Inc., 1983), 120.

The case appeared to be a first—a *Salmonella* epidemic caused by contaminated marijuana.

David N. Taylor, et al, "Salmonellosis Associated With Marijuana," *The New England Journal of Medicine*, 27 May 1982, 1249–1253.

Chapter Eight

In 1985, there had been only 22,000 new cases of TB . . .

Michael Specter, "Neglected for Years, TB Is Back," *The New York Times*, 11 October 1992.

New York City hospitals that once supported a total of one thousand beds . . .

Michael Specter, "Neglected for Years, TB Is Back," *The New York Times*, 11 October 1992.

"We've not been too wise over the years,"

Dr. Dixie Snider, director of the Division of Tuberculosis Control at the CDC, quoted in Andrew Purvis, "TB Takes a Deadly Turn," *Time*, 2 December 1991, 85.

. . . people infected with the AIDS virus made up at least 25 percent of the city's new TB cases every year.

Terence Monmaney, "The Return of Tuberculosis," *Newsweek*, 22 February 1988, 68.

"They do it one way at Columbia [medical school]. Another at Cornell. I have my own . . . mix. We really need . . . better guidance."

Dr. Eran Bellin, quoted in Elisabeth Rosenthal, "Doctors and Patients Are Pushed to Their Limits," *The New York Times*, 12 October 1992.

"Think about it, it makes sense."

Dr. Michael Iseman, quoted in Elisabeth Rosenthal, "Doctors and Patients Are Pushed to Their Limits," *The New York Times*, 12 October 1992.

" . . . When people are scared they grab for a simple answer. And locking sick people away is a simple answer. Simple, quick and wrong."

Dr. Thomas Frieden, Director of N.Y. Bureau of TB Control, quoted in Michael Specter, "TB Carriers See Clash of Liberty and Health," *The New York Times*, 14 October 1992.

New York City claimed it would raise at least $100 million to be spent on TB in 1993. The Federal government planned to set aside only $74.3 million for the rest of the nation for that same period.

Michael Specter, "Neglected for Years, TB Is Back," *The New York Times*, 11 October 1992.

"It's a winnable battle. . . . We know what has to be done. We just don't know whether we as a society will be able to do it."

Dr. Thomas Frieden, quoted in Ken Chowder, "How TB Survived Its Own Death To Confront Us Again," *Smithsonian*, November 1992, 194.

Chapter Nine

(The McDevitts' story is also recounted in Jean Block's article, "The Accident That Saved Five Lives.")

"I guess we all have a touch of the flu . . ."

Dr. Thomas McDevitt, quoted in Jean Libman Block, "The Accident That Saved Five Lives," *Good Housekeeping*, November 1969, 51–70.

"Dr. McDevitt, you and your daughter are severely anemic . . .", "You have just about reached your limit . . .", and "Get out of your house . . ."

Dr. Fishkin, Chief Pathologist, quoted in Jean Libman Block, "The Accident That Saved Five Lives," *Good Housekeeping*, November 1969, 51–70.

"Pure lead chromate . . ."

Dr. H. N. Broderson, District Health Officer Santa Monica Public Health Department, quoted in Jean Libman Block, "The Accident That Saved Five Lives," *Good Housekeeping*, November 1969, 51–70.

Chapter Ten

"In each case we asked ourselves what they died from, and the answer was 'Nothing.'"

> James Essling, Chief Investigator for St. Paul's Medical Examiner, Ramsey Co., Minn., quoted in David Monagan, "Curse of the Sleeping Death," *Science Digest*, April 1982, 36.

By July 1985, more than eighty cases were recorded in the United States.

> "Ailing Arrivals," *Scientific American*, July 1985, 58–60.

October 1987 brought the total to over one hundred . . .

> "Sudden Refugee Death," *Natural History*, October 1987, 4–6.

"We are in the process of describing . . ."

> Dr. Roy Baron, CDC, quoted in David Monagan, "Curse of the Sleeping Death," *Science Digest*, April 1982, 36.

Glossary

AIDS. Acquired Immune Deficiency Syndrome: an infectious, transmissible disease in which the body's immune system is damaged, leaving the person vulnerable to a number of secondary infections and cancers.

Anemia. A condition in which there is a reduction in the number of red blood cells that carry oxygen to body tissues, resulting in paleness or generalized weakness.

Antibiotic. Any of a variety of chemical substances, such as penicillin or tetracycline, that have the ability to destroy or slow the growth of bacteria or other microorganisms.

Antibodies. Substances produced by the body to help it fight against a specific disease, toxin, or other foreign substance.

Apnea. A temporary halt in breathing, often related to snoring, that produces irregular heartbeats.

Arthritis. A chronic disease characterized by inflammation, swelling, and pain of the joints.

Autopsy. Examination of a body to determine the cause of death.

Bacteria (sing. bacterium). Single-cell organisms, some disease-causing, that have no chlorophyll, multiply by simple division, and can be seen only with a microscope; they occur in three main forms; spherical, rod-shaped, and spiral.

Bulbar poliomyelitis. The most serious form of poliomyelitis (polio), an infectious disease of the brain and spinal cord, caused by a virus. In bulbar polio, the virus can damage nerve cells in the brain that control swallowing, breathing, and facial movement.

CAT scan. Computerized Axial Tomography; X ray combined with computer analysis that provides detailed pictures of parts of the body including the brain, spine, lungs, pancreas, and liver. CAT scans are useful in detecting tumors, cysts, organ damage, and similar abnormalities.

Centers for Disease Control and Prevention (CDC). Known as the Centers for Disease Control until October 27, 1992; agency with branches across the country, responsible for researching health problems and working to control and prevent disease throughout the United States.

Coma. A state of deep, continued unconsciousness, caused by injury or disease.

Contagious. Capable of being passed from person to person.

Contaminate. To make impure or infected.

Debilitate. To make weak or feeble.

Diabetes. A disorder in which the body cannot break down or utilize sugar, resulting in a buildup of dangerous amounts of sugar in the blood.

Drug-resistance. The ability to be largely unaffected by certain drugs or medications.

Epidemic. An abnormally high number of cases of a disease.

Epidemic Intelligence Service (EIS). Part of the Centers for Disease Control, specializing in finding the cause of epidemic diseases and preventing their spread.

Eradicate. To get rid of; to destroy.

Fungi (sing. fungus). Simple plants, often microscopic and disease-producing, that feed on tissues of living or dead plants and animals. Fungi lack chlorophyll, true roots, stems, and leaves, and reproduce by means of spores.

Goiter. An enlargement of the thyroid gland, often visible as a swelling on the front of the neck.

Hantavirus. One of a group of viruses, first discovered in the Far East, named after the Han River in South Korea. The most famous member of the group, the Hantaan virus, can cause uncontrolled bleeding and kidney failure in humans.

Immune system. White blood cells that help defend the body against disease, toxins, or other foreign substances. Lymphocytes are produced in the bone marrow and help form antibodies. Macrophages, larger cells found in the liver, lymph glands, and bone marrow, surround harmful invaders and digest them.

Immunosuppression. A condition in which the body's immune system is inactivated through medication or disease, leaving the body with little or no resistance to infection.

Incubation time. The period in the development of a disease between the time disease organisms enter the victim and the first appearance of symptoms.

Intravenous. Directly into a vein.

Juvenile rheumatoid arthritis. A chronic disease, affecting children, whose cause is unknown. The condition involves inflammation, pain, and swelling of the joints, as well as damage to organs and connective tissue.

Latent. Lying hidden or undeveloped within a person or thing.

Lethal. Capable of causing death.

Lymphatic system. A network of small vessels, similar to blood vessels, that returns fluid from body tissues to the blood. Lymph glands, part of the same network, produce cells that help fight infection in the body.

Malnutrition. Poor nourishment resulting from too little food or improper diet.

Microbe. A microscopic organism.

Microbiologist. A scientist who studies microorganisms such as bacteria and viruses.

Mutation. An abrupt and relatively permanent change in some inheritable characteristic of a cell.

National Institutes of Health (NIH). The United States agency, and its branches, that supports medical research in such areas as allergy, aging, cancer, and the environment. About 40 percent of all health research in the United States is financed by the NIH.

Neurosurgeon. A doctor specializing in surgery involving some part of the nervous system, including the brain and spinal cord.

Opportunistic infection. An illness caused by a bacterium, virus, or parasite that produces symptoms only in people with weakened or deficient immune systems.

Pathogen. Any microorganism or virus that can cause disease.

Pathologist. A doctor specializing in the cause and nature of diseases.

Quarantine. Any isolation or restriction on travel imposed to keep contagious diseases from spreading.

Resuscitate. To revive or bring back to life.

Retrovirus. A virus that invades a cell and then reverses the usual process by which the cell copies its genetic code.

Rheumatic fever. A disease that sometimes follows an infection by *Streptococcus* bacteria; symptoms include fever, pain, swelling of the joints, and inflammation of the heart.

Rickettsias (sing. rickettsia). Single-cell microorganisms, now regarded as a type of bacteria, that cause diseases such as typhus and Rocky Mountain spotted fever. Rickettsias differ from bacteria in two major ways: they are smaller, and they cannot reproduce outside of living cells.

Salmonellosis. Commonly known as food poisoning; a disease caused by the *Salmonella* bacteria. Symptoms include fever and intestinal disorders.

Shigellosis. Commonly known as dysentary; a disease caused by the *Shigella* bacteria. Symptoms include abdominal pain and diarrhea.

Spirochete. Any of a group of slender, corkscrew-shaped bacteria that move with a twisting motion. Some cause disease, some are parasitic, others are free-living.

T-helper cells. Part of the immune system; white blood cells, also known as lymphocytes, that mature in the thymus gland and assist in the production of antibodies.

Toxin. Any of various poisons.

Vaccine. Any preparation of dead microorganisms or weakened living organisms introduced into the body to help build protection against disease.

Virus. Ultramicroscopic infective agents that cause various diseases in plants and animals. A virus is capable of multiplying only in connection with living cells.

For Further Reading

Aaseng, Nathan. *The Disease Fighters*. Minneapolis: Lerner Publications, 1987.

Astor, Gerald. *The Disease Detectives*. New York: New American Library, Inc., 1983.

Berger, Melvin. *Disease Detectives*. New York: Thomas Y. Crowell, 1978.

Biel, Timothy L., Maurie Manning, and Michael Spackman. *The Black Death*. San Diego: Lucent Books, 1989.

Birch, Beverly. *Louis Pasteur*. Milwaukee: Gareth Stevens Children's Books, 1989.

Fradin, Dennis Brindell. *Medicine: Yesterday, Today and Tomorrow*. Chicago: Childrens Press, 1989.

Knight, David C. *Viruses, Life's Smallest Enemies*. New York: William Morrow & Co., 1981.

Landau, Elaine. *Lyme Disease*. New York: Franklin Watts, 1990.

Levert, Suzanne. *AIDS: In Search of a Killer.* New York: Simon & Schuster, Inc., 1987.

Nardo, Don. *Germs, Mysterious Microorganisms.* San Diego: Lucent Books, 1991.

Roueché, Berton. *The Medical Detectives.* New York: Times Books, 1981.

Silverstein, Alvin, and Virginia Silverstein. *AIDS: Deadly Threat.* Hillside, N.J.: Enslow Publishers, Inc., 1991.

Index

Black Death, 62, 63, 70, *71*
Blastomycosis, 19
Blood transfusions, 48
Borrelia burgdorferi, 30
Brantley, Jerry, 43, 44
Bright, Donald, 35, 37, 38, 41
Bubonic plague, 19, 64
Bulbar poliomyelitis, 33
Burgdorfer, Willy, 30
Butyl nitrate, 48

Campbell, Ernest, 16
Cancer, 60
Candidiasis (thrush), 42, 43, 46
Carlsbad cave bats, 40
Carlson, Jan, 25–26, 31
CAT scan (Computerized Axial Tomography), 92
Cavana, Johnny, 52–60
Centers for Disease Control and Prevention (CDC), 12–13, 16, 19–21, 28, 38, 40, 44–47, 64, 65, 68, 70, 72, 83, 99, 102
Ceramic glaze, *94*, 96, 97
Charcoal yeast extract agar, 23
Chicken pox, 70
Cholera, 12
Conrad, John, Jr., 53–59
Curran, James, 44, 45

Darby, Ken, 42–43
Deer ticks, 26, 29, *30*
Diabetes, 52, 93
Drug resistance, 85, 88, 89

Drugs, 48, 77–79, *78*

Ebola fever, 12
Epidemic Intelligence Service (EIS) officers, 16
Erythromycin, 23
Ettenger, Molly, 62, 64

Fleas, 63, 65, 66, 69
Flu, 21, 69, 70
Food and Drug Administration (FDA), 97
Food poisoning, 72–79
Foxes, 41
Fraser, David, 16, 18–20, 22, 23
Frieden, Thomas, 87, 89
Fungi, 18, 19

Gallo, Robert, 49–51
Genital herpes, 48
Gonorrhea, 48
Gottlieb, Michael, 42–44

Haitian refugees, 48, 49
Hanna, Duke, 92
Hantaviruses, 69–70
Hemophiliacs, 48
Hidden killers
    AIDS (Acquired Immune Deficiency Syndrome), 42–51, *94*
    food poisoning, 72–79
    lead poisoning, 90–93, 95–97
    Legionnaires' disease, 15, 16, 18–24, 69
    Lyme disease, 25–32

Taylor, David, 72–79
T-helper cells, 43, 45, 49
Ticks, 26, 29, *30*
Tilson, Hank, 34, 35, 41
Tilson, Marybelle, 33–34, 38, 41
Toxic substances, 18–19 (*see also* Food poisoning; Lead poisoning; Pesticide poisoning)
Toxoplasmosis, 46
Trujillo, Sammy, 67
Tuberculosis (TB), 12, 80–85, *82*, *86*, 87–89
Typhoid, 19

Unexplained adult respiratory-distress syndrome, 68

Vampire bats, 35, 40
Viruses, 18, 19, 30, 34

Warren, Merritt, 58
Water pipes, 95, 97
Weisman, Joel, 43
World Health Organization (WHO), 46

Yamaguchi, Tiyo, 57–59
Yersin, Alexandre É. J., 63
Yersinia pestis, 63, 64, 66

DATE			